When Mormons Call

Answering Mormon Missionaries at Your Door

ISAIAH BENNETT

When Mormons Call

*Answering Mormon
Missionaries at Your Door*

CATHOLIC ANSWERS
SAN DIEGO
1999

Unless otherwise noted, Scripture quotations taken from the *King James Version* (KJV) of the Bible.

Other Scripture quotations taken from the *New American Bible* (NAB) © 1969–1986, Confraternity of Christian Doctrine, or from the *Revised Standard Version* (RSV) © 1946–1957, Division of Christian Education of the National Council of the Churches of Christ in the United States of America, from the *New International Version* (NIV) © 1973–1984, International Bible Society.

Published by Catholic Answers, Inc.
P.O. Box 17490
San Diego, California 92177
(888) 291–8000 (U.S. orders)
(619) 541–1131 (int'l. orders)
(619) 541–1154 (fax)
www.catholic.com (web)

Cover design by Kray Marketing
Printed in the United States of America
ISBN 1–888992–07–7

In honor of
Our Lady of Perpetual Help

Contents

Abbreviations

The following abbreviations are used throughout the book:

1. Mormon Texts

CR   *Conference Reports*, general conference talks by Mormon authorities.

D&C   Doctrine and Covenants, Mormon scriptures written by Joseph Smith and others.

DS   *Doctrines of Salvation*, Joseph Fielding Smith.

EM   *Encyclopedia of Mormonism*, published in 1992.

HC   *History of the Church*, by Joseph Smith and others.

JD   *Journal of Discourses*, writings and sermons by Brigham Young and early Mormon leaders.

MD   *Mormon Doctrine*, Bruce R. McConkie.

TPJS   *Teachings of the Prophet Joseph Smith*, Joseph Fielding Smith.

2. Catholic Texts

CCC   *Catechism of the Catholic Church*, 1994.

CF   *Catholicism and Fundamentalism*, Karl Keating, 1988.

IM   *Inside Mormonism: What Mormons Really Believe*, Isaiah Bennett, 1999.

TB   *Theology for Beginners*, Frank J. Sheed, 1981.

ONE

The Discussions

1. Mormon Methods
—an Overview

Meeting the Missionaries

There are a number of ways you could meet Mormon missionaries:

1. They come, uninvited, to your door. They're out "tracting" in your neighborhood and they take a chance you'll be home.

2. You see one of the Mormon church's slick ads on TV and call for a free video, Book of Mormon or Bible. Generally, these giveaways come with two missionaries attached.

3. A Mormon acquaintance alerts the missionaries, giving them your name and address with the hope that their message appeals to you.

At the Door

They're not inside your house, yet. But maybe it's raining or scorching hot or bone-numbing cold. And the poor guys are on bikes. Your compassionate Catholic heart goes out to them.

But wait. Have you asked them to visit? Or did they show up unexpected? Are they "just in the neighborhood today" to "share the gospel"? Are they delivering a video you thought you were getting with "no strings attached"? Could you have agreed, under pressure, to let one of your Mormon friends send them?

Think hard! If you let them in and listen to their presentation, you've taken the first step they want you to take. A foot in the door is all that's needed, and the young missionaries have been well trained to make that move.

Quick Reactions

Rather than let them in (especially if they weren't invited), be polite. Say, "Thank you for stopping by (and leaving the tape, book or whatever). We're a Catholic family and have no interest in hearing your presentation." Then say it again. And again. Missionaries don't easily accept "No." You might also have handy a tract or holy card presenting a Catholic prayer or doctrinal explanation. Trade that for whatever they want to leave with you.

This scenario applies to the young "elders" or "sisters"[1] who come to your door. But Mormons also proselytize during casual contacts with friends or acquaintances. Mormon leaders have made it clear that each member is to seek potential recruits. It's part of their work to "spread the gospel" to every person.

The Mormon Faith Is Based on Feelings

Mormons say they are "Spirit-led." That is, their personal beliefs are based to a large extent on their subjective "testimonies" or feelings that a teaching or practice is true. Never mind that one Mormon teaching may be inconsistent with another or that a doctrine once taught as God's revealed law is now denied and demeaned. Never mind what scientific or rational analysis may disclose: If I "feel" a thing to be true, then it's true. Facts will not convince me to turn from my subjective testimony. If I believe the Holy Ghost has told me, interiorly, what is true, how can I deny him by listening to his enemies, such as history, science, and the whole

---

[1] Mormons refer to the young men sent on missions as "elders." Most are not yet twenty. Women are referred to as "sisters." In Mormon circles, this is not a term used for nuns, which they do not have.

of lost Christianity? The choice, for the Mormon, is clear: either God and the Mormon church or their satanic detractors.

By being encouraged to "feel" led by the Spirit, a potential convert can deal with any opposition leveled at him or the church by well-intentioned but "misguided and blind" relatives, friends, and pastors, who are, in varying degrees, under the devil's sway. Their resistance, the missionaries teach, displeases the Lord and hinders his "one, true" church.

This is why the young elders or sisters who try to convert you are usually unaffected by evidence you present contradicting their programmed discussions. They have been taught to distrust anything not Mormon. They interpret any criticism of their beliefs as persecution and call anyone who questions their tenets "anti-Mormon," even if the disapproval is sincere and polite.

From a Christian perspective, Christ said the "truth" will set us free (John 8:32). He did not tell us to "feel" our way into his Church. To know him—he is the "truth" (John 14:6)—and his will, we are to seek (Matt. 7:7) and study, to search his word in Scripture and the Church's teaching authority (Acts 17:10–11) and to listen to his chosen leaders, for that is the same as listening to him (Luke 10:16).

Preliminary Do's and Don'ts

1. Before discussing faith with anyone, be sure to know, love, and practice your own. You don't have to be a religious expert with an answer to every problem that's raised. But you do need to have a firm understanding of the teachings of the Catholic Church, their foundations in reason, Scripture and Tradition, and a desire to live a life committed to Christ.

2. You also need inner peace. If there are elements in your personal or emotional life that have opened you up to

depression, resentment or confusion, tend to those first, through prayer and proper counseling.[2]

3. When confronted, either formally by missionaries or casually by Mormon acquaintances, show them Christ's love and care. He loves them just as he loves you. Don't slam the door in their face or call them names. This is not Christ-like and only feeds their belief that they're persecuted because they alone work for God.

4. Mormons are told to refer any possible "investigators" to the official missionaries, who will then teach a prepared set of six lessons. The discussions are inoffensive and superficial. Presenting you with the weightier Mormon beliefs is not encouraged: It could scare you off. Don't allow the missionaries to control the conversation. It's your future (and your eternal destiny) that are involved.

5. After having studied beforehand a particular topic in this book, stay with it. Don't let the missionaries give a quick brush-off and change the subject. Remember, they learned in their training course to "build" on each item they present. To deflect them from the pre-arranged flow could unsettle and confuse them. That's all right. They need to be shaken up and encouraged to think for themselves.

6. Don't try to answer a question they may raise about the Catholic faith if you're unsure how to. Tell them you'll research it. This book is a good place to start, especially with the suggested readings offered at the end of each topic.

---

[2] This was, I think, my problem. Though I had always known, loved, and tried to practice my Catholic faith, interior pains made me particularly vulnerable to the simplistic "solutions" often offered by Mormonism and other sects. This led to the time I spent as a Mormon, before my eventual, joyous return to the Catholic faith.

7. If you're prepared to confront the Mormon on a major point, stay with it. Don't allow him to divert you with, "Well, what about . . ."

8. Refuse to be persuaded by the missionary's "testimony." Yes, they are usually clean-cut, polite, and earnest. But what salesman comes to your door disheveled and obnoxious? Many are sincere. But not all. And many lose their "testimony" during or shortly after their one and one-half or two years of full-time church work.

9. Respond to their testimony by bearing your own. You know the truth of your own faith, too, and you can back it up with something beyond mere sentiment. The Catholic Christian faith has serious, objective evidence on its side. Mormonism does not. By pointing to this objective evidence, you counter their purely subjective "testimony."

10. When asked to pick someone to offer a beginning or closing prayer, choose yourself and make it a Catholic prayer (the Our Father, Hail Mary, Glory Be, for example). Don't forget to make the sign of the cross. Don't feel that you have to accommodate your prayers to them: They asked you to do the picking. Do so in accordance with your Catholic faith.

11. If the missionaries want to leave you a copy of the Book of Mormon or some other Mormon pamphlet, make no commitment to read it. Instead, have something handy to give them, and ask them for their own promise to read and pray about it. Only if they do so might you agree to see them again.

12. If you engage in an extended discussion with the missionaries, I suggest you ask them about the so-called "Great Apostasy." Even though this topic is not broached until the third discussion, it is the linchpin of Mormonism's existence. If the Christian Church did not completely

defect in the early centuries after Christ, there would be no need for Mormonism's founder, Joseph Smith, to "restore" it early in the nineteenth century. The Mormon church would therefore be wrong and superfluous.

13. Finally, I repeat: Do none of the above if you're unsure of the first and second points.

Mormon Missionary Strategy

Mormon missionaries try to convert people by offering a structured series of six "discussions" designed to skim the surface of complex and contradictory Mormon beliefs. Missionaries have been trained to present the topics of these discussions and not to stray from them. These classes last about an hour each and are generally scheduled in the investigator's home. Depending on the zeal of the missionaries and the susceptibility of the potential convert, the talks could be completed in a month or so, or dragged out indefinitely.

Using this Handbook

In section 2, twenty-five of the major themes presented in the missionary discussions are analyzed. I provide you with the standard Mormon teaching, together with a Christian (and specifically, Catholic) response. In many cases, you also will learn of related doctrines and practices the missionaries withhold from you in their official presentation. (For example, the idea that God the Father and Mary engaged in physical, sexual intercourse to produce the mortal Jesus Christ.) Learn the section 2 topics thoroughly and you will be prepared to answer Mormon claims when missionaries come to your door. For a more thorough examination of the same topics, see my book *Inside Mormonism: What Mormons Really Believe* (San Diego: Catholic Answers, 1999).

Unless otherwise noted, all biblical references are to the King James Version of the Bible, the only version accepted by the Mormon church. You may want to consult a more correct translation (such as the Revised Standard Version—Catholic Edition) to help you understand the KJV's somewhat stilted and confusing language.

In what follows, I have cited only "authoritative" Mormon leaders and theologians. While there is widespread dissension in the Mormon church today, I have tried to present fairly the common doctrines held (or once held) by the general membership.

2. The Six Missionary Discussions—an Overview

Discussion One:
"The Plan of Our Heavenly Father"

In this lesson, the missionaries will tell you: God has a plan for our salvation. Since we are his children, we are to become like him. Jesus has a central mission in this plan. By his resurrection we can live again. By faith and by following the Lord's perfect example, we can return to God and live forever. We find out about this divine plan through prophets, who continue to teach even today. Joseph Smith is one such prophet; indeed, he is the greatest. He had a vision as a young boy and was used by God to bring back the true Christian church. He did this, in part, by discovering and translating the Book of Mormon, an ancient record of Hebrew people living in America. You can know that what the missionaries say is true by listening to their "testimonies" and praying to receive one of your own.

The elders ask the investigator to make a number of "commitments": Read portions of the Book of Mormon and pray about it, allow them to return for the next discussion and consider being baptized into The Church of Jesus Christ of Latter-day Saints.

This first discussion presents a huge amount of material. Consult the section 2 topics relevant to this first discussion. Most importantly, read chapter 16, "Joseph Smith," first. The life of Joseph Smith is the key to understanding Mormon history and belief. (While the chapters in section 2 serve to correct Mormon errors, the treatment of God, the First Vision, and the Book of Mormon are most important.) The relevant section 2 topics for this discussion are: Plan of Salvation, God, Jesus Christ, Prophets, First Vision, Book of Mormon, the Holy Ghost, and Prayer.

Discussion Two:
"The Gospel of Jesus Christ"

In this lesson, the missionaries will tell you: Jesus Christ overcame physical death by his resurrection. Therefore, all people will be resurrected. To be saved from sin, we must use our free agency (free will), accept Christ and follow the Mormon faith. Faith in Christ means serving him; repentance is total and permanent commitment to the Mormon gospel. The outward expression of this is Mormon baptism. With this "ordinance" (Mormons use this term, not "sacrament"), we receive the companionship of the Holy Ghost. By obeying God's commandments as taught by the Mormon church, and by enduring to the end, we can be saved.

The listener is now asked to commit to a date for Mormon baptism. The potential convert may have had only a week or so exposure to the church, yet he's asked to make a total and permanent dedication of his self and his future to an institution he knows next to nothing about. That Mormonism's Christ is not the same Christ of the Bible, the apostles, and the early Church is clear from the topic on Jesus Christ.

The relevant section 2 topics for this discussion are: Jesus Christ, Atonement, Baptism, and the Holy Ghost.

Discussion Three:
"The Restoration"

In this lesson, the missionaries will tell you: We must find and accept the truth. By doing this, we learn that Christ founded his Church by revelation. It is continued today by "apostles" and "prophets." But it was not always so. The first apostles were rejected and their priestly authority was completely lost. Therefore, for centuries, the institution known as "Christendom" was in reality an apostate church opposed to God and the truth. Not until 1830, when Joseph Smith organized the Mormon church, was the true church of Christ restored to a lost world. Priestly authority was re-established. New scriptures were brought forth and ancient rituals were again performed. An outward indication of membership in the one, true church is weekly attendance at its meetings.

This time, the listener is asked to commit to Sunday meetings. He's also asked to strengthen his promise to be baptized and also to give the missionaries names of family members or friends who may be contacted for conversion.

Essential to the entire Mormon program is the notion of a complete apostasy. Study that topic thoroughly. The relevant section 2 topics for this discussion are: Apostasy, The Church, Priesthood, Meetings, and Standard Works.

Discussion Four:
"Eternal Progression"

In this lesson, the missionaries will tell you: Each one of us lived with God the Father and our "Heavenly Mother" (a wife of God the Father) in the eons before we were conceived by our earthly parents. When we finally took on a physical body, we were given the opportunity to accept the Mormon plan, live obediently and finally progress to godhood ourselves. Only temple-worthy Mormons can become gods. Non-Mormons and those who fall short of the ideal do not return to God the Father. Genealogy and proxy work for the dead are necessary if they, too, are to be saved. Families can thus be "for ever." Chastity and obedience to such rules as the "Word of Wisdom" are also necessary for eventual godhood.

Commitments at this stage include living chastely (taught by most faiths) and keeping the Word of Wisdom.

Many people are intrigued by the Mormon temples, though they know little of what goes on behind their doors. Though Mormons keep it "secret," it's not all that mysterious. In fact, it's banal and repetitive. (Take it from one who's been through Mormon temple work.) Considering you have to be a very good

Mormon for at least a year before you can enter, it's not worth all the time, effort, and money you have to spend to earn entrance.

The relevant section 2 topics for this discussion are: Plan of Salvation, Chastity and Sexual Morality, Families, Word of Wisdom, Temples, and Three Degrees of Glory.

Discussion Five:
"Living a Christ-like Life"

In this lesson, the missionaries will tell you: God requires sacrifice, which in turn brings us blessings. We show our love for him by following his commands and by service to others. (Most faiths teach the same.) Fasting and tithing are two ways we show our faith in God's loving care. The potential convert is asked to give ten percent of his income to the Mormon church. Such tithing is a prerequisite for temple attendance and church standing. The relevant section 2 topic for this discussion is: Tithing.

Discussion Six:
"Membership in the Kingdom"

In this lesson, the missionaries will tell you the following: Jesus Christ is the Creator, Redeemer, and Judge. Through obedience to his Mormon church, we can attain "exaltation," or the highest level of salvation. We become gods of our own worlds. The Mormon church's mission, therefore, is to help "perfect the saints, proclaim the gospel, and redeem the dead." We must heed the inspired guidance of Mormon leaders, follow the scriptures, perform the ordinances and serve. Spreading the Mormon message is crucial to our own advancement, so we must cultivate a missionary spirit. Finally, by researching our family trees and performing proxy temple work for our dead ancestors, we enable them to become Mormons (and gods) too.

Those who have uncritically participated in the missionary discussions thus far may find themselves on the brink of Mormon baptism (or may have already taken the plunge at the hands of eager elders). Their final commitment is to obey the Mormon church in all things. They must now believe its contradictory doctrines, follow its non-Christian practices and abandon their demonstrably higher Catholic moral standards. This is what the missionaries hope for. It is the reason they spend time engaging in these discussions.

The relevant section 2 topics for this discussion are: Jesus Christ, Prophets, Continuous Revelation, Missionary Work, Genealogy, and Three Degrees of Glory.

TWO

The Topics

3. Apostasy

(Use for Discussion 3)

According to the Mormon church, the Catholic Church and all Protestant churches constitute a fallen, apostate Christendom. Joseph Smith said, "I have more to boast of than any other man. I am the only man that has ever been able to keep a whole church together since the days of Adam. A large majority of the whole have stood by me. Neither Paul, John, Peter, nor Jesus ever did it. I boast that no man ever did such a work as I. The followers of Jesus ran away from Him; but the Latter-day Saints never ran away from me yet" (*HC* 6:408–409).

His bragging was premature. Before his death while participating in a gun battle at age thirty-eight, in 1844, most of his original colleagues had either left the Mormon church or had been excommunicated. Upon his death, several splinter groups emerged, all claiming his prophetic mantle. Many endure to this day.

The Process of Apostasy

Mormon theology holds that Christ established his true Church during his earthly ministry. He founded it in Palestine first and then, after his ascension, came to the Americas and established it again among the Jewish immigrants he found there.

Mormons claim that, even during the lives of the original twelve apostles, conspiring, influential men began to infect the Church with their pagan philosophies and their hunger for power. Weakened by persecutions and corrupted by Greek and other "non-biblical" doctrines, the Christian Church fell away gradually, though completely. It was replaced, certainly by the third or fourth century, with Catholicism, the state religion.

The "great and abominable church," "the church of Satan," had replaced true Christianity. The priesthood, which Mormons define as the power and authority to act in God's name, was lost from the earth. All sacraments or ordinances were thus invalid and, according to some Mormon theologians, works of the devil.

From the Mormon perspective, the sixteenth-century Protestant Reformation addressed some problems. But, since there was no valid authority in the Catholic Church from which the reformers broke, they themselves were devoid of the priesthood needed to teach and minister according to Christ's original plan. So the whole world continued in darkness. (The church founded by the Lord in the New World had also fallen away.)

Then, in 1820, the Mormon church claims, God appeared to a farm boy in upstate New York. Ten years later, Smith organized his church.

No Apostasy Means
No Reason for a Restoration

The Mormon church is not a reformation of doctrine and practice. It cannot be called yet another Protestant sect, though it is highly influenced by Smith's Protestant heritage. Rather, it claims to be a radical restoration of the Church first established by Christ but fallen into apostasy. Nothing short of a bringing-back of the true Church, with its priesthood and ordinances, would be enough to give the world a true knowledge of God and the means to reach him.

Mormons acknowledge that only a restoration could repair a total apostasy. In addition, they admit that no restoration was needed unless there had been a total apostasy. The entire basis for the Mormon church crumbles if it fails to produce proof of a total, universal falling away of the early Church.

Many Mormon doctrines were unknown to or repudiated by Christians from the time of the apostles to the present. By showing that pure doctrine and valid authority have existed in the

Church throughout its twenty centuries, you can show the Mormon missionary the impossibility of a general apostasy. The Mormon church's attempts to restore teachings and practices are, then, actually attacks on the faith "once for all delivered unto the saints" (Jude 3).

Bible Verses Mormons Use

Trying to substantiate their claim of a total apostasy, the Mormon church looks to several scriptural verses:

> Let no man deceive you by any means: for that day shall not come, except there come a falling away first, and that man of sin be revealed, the son of perdition [2 Thess. 2:3].

> For there shall arise false Christs, and false prophets, and shall shew great signs and wonders; insomuch that, if it were possible, they shall deceive the very elect [Matt. 24:11].

> For I know this, that after my departing shall grievous wolves enter in among you, not sparing the flock [Acts 20:29–30].

> I marvel that ye are so soon removed from him that called you into the grace of Christ unto another gospel. . . . But though we, or an angel from heaven, preach any other gospel unto you than that which we have preached unto you, let him be accursed [Gal. 1:6, 8].

> Also, Isaiah 29:13; Amos 8:11–12; Ephesians 4:14; 1 Timothy 1:5–7, 4:1–3; 2 Timothy 2:18, 3:1–7, 4:3–4; 2 Peter 2:1–2.

Not one of these references indicates a total apostasy. It is true that some who professed to be followers of Christ introduced false doctrines and led lives unworthy of their baptism. This is not a surprise to anyone familiar with the weakness of his own human nature.

Yes, there would be some, even in positions of authority, who would abuse their gifts and lead others astray with them. We were warned about that in advance. Individual apostasies will continue as long as man has the freedom to serve God or self. But the true Church endures. Mormons fail to produce even one citation describing or prophesying anything but partial and individual apostasies.

Bible Verses Indicating a Permanent Church

On the other hand, Catholics find ample scriptural basis for their belief in the indefectibility of the Church.

And I say also unto thee, That thou art Peter, and upon this rock I will build my church; and the gates of hell shall not prevail against it [Matt. 16:18].

Teaching them to observe all things whatsoever I have commanded you: and, lo, I am with you alway [sic], even unto the end of the world [Matt. 28:20].

And I will pray the Father, and he shall give you another Comforter, that he may abide with you for ever [John 14:16].

It is inconceivable that Christ, God Almighty, would make promises he either couldn't fulfill or knew he wouldn't be allowed to. If his Church were to fall away so soon after its institution, why assure it that he would be with it always? Why send the Holy Spirit, only to have him depart well before "the end of the world"? If the Church indeed rejected God and his priesthood and lost all means of saving grace, then the gates of hell *would* have prevailed against it.

Two other images of the Church in the New Testament help us see its intimate connection with its Lord.

The following verses depict the Church as God's house, planned and built with foresight and care. With its solid foundation and immovable cornerstone, it is a "strong man's" house designed to last through "all ages:" Luke 14:28–30; Mark 3:27; 1 Timothy 3:15; Hebrews 11:10; 1 Peter 2:6; 1 Corinthians 3:11; Luke 1:32–33; Ephesians 3:21.

The Church is also the Body of Christ, with Jesus as its head. It is he who nourishes it and cares for it, feeding it on his word and his flesh. His Holy Spirit, once bestowed, gives it life eternal: Romans 12:5; Colossians 1:18; Ephesians 1:22, 5:29. Even Old Testament prophets knew Christ's kingdom would have no end, could not be destroyed. (The Mormon church's own Bible version footnotes the following two passages as references to Christ and his Church.)

> For unto us a child is born, unto us a son is given: and the government shall be upon his shoulder. . . . Of the increase of his government and peace there shall be no end, upon the throne of David, and upon his kingdom [Is. 9:6–7].

> I saw in the night visions, and, behold, one like the Son of man came with the clouds of heaven, and came to the Ancient of days, and they brought him near before him. And there was given him dominion, and glory, and a kingdom, that all people, nations, and languages, should serve him: his dominion is an everlasting dominion, which shall not pass away, and his kingdom that which shall not be destroyed [Dan. 7:13–14].

Mormons must prove from the Bible that a total apostasy was predicted. They may not refer to their own scriptures, such as the Book of Mormon, for proof. Citing corrupt Church leaders is irrelevant. An individual or group, no matter how many or how highly placed, does not constitute the Lord's Church.[1] The

---

[1] Even a pope can err. Peter did and was rebuked by Paul (Gal. 2:11–16), yet

Catholic Church has endured from the time of Christ not because of the failings of its members, but in spite of them.

Further reading: *CCC* 748–870; *CF*, chapters 17, 18 and 23; *IM*, chapters 9–16; *TB*, chapter 13.

---

he was still a valid pope. He went on to write two inspired works of Scripture —1 and 2 Peter.

4. Atonement

(*Use for Discussion 2*)

The Mormon church occasionally preaches a doctrine as if only its own members believed it. The atonement of Christ is a case in point. Mormons point to such passages as the Book of Mormon's Alma 34:8–9 as indicators that they alone teach the truth about the Lord's work of redemption. It doesn't seem to occur to many Mormons that traditional Christianity has always professed the necessity and reality of Christ's saving work on the cross. No Book of Mormon passage needs to be added to the clear testimony of the Bible.

Levels of Salvation

Mormons err, however, in splitting the idea of "salvation" into two levels. First, the Mormon church teaches that, because of Christ's atonement, all people will be raised from the dead, regardless of their earthly merits. Christ conquered death, so all men will rise. This is the "general" salvation.

Second, "individual" salvation, or salvation in the full sense, is given to those whose earthly lives merit it. This is an earned salvation consisting of several degrees or levels.

Forgiveness of Sins

Christ's sufferings in Gethsemane and death on Calvary made possible the forgiveness of our sins. Absolution is based on thorough repentance and amendment of life. But not all who sincerely repent and try to live a good life avoid future failures. Mormon prophets make it clear that future sins bring back the guilt and penalty of earlier, repented sins: "Each previously forgiven sin is added to the new one and the whole gets to be a heavy load" (Spencer W. Kimball, *The Miracle of Forgiveness*, 170).

The Atonement of Christ Can't Cover Some Sins

A Mormon doctrine nowhere mentioned in the missionary discussions, the notion of "blood atonement" has existed from the earliest years of the church up to the present. The assumption is this: While Christ's atonement provides forgiveness for the vast majority of sins, there are some transgressions that even his death is incapable of remitting. The only hope for salvation in these cases lies in the sinner having his own blood shed as a personal atonement.

Two such categories are murderers and certain apostates from the Mormon church. In the past, church leaders also included adulterers, thieves, and those who married blacks. Utah and Idaho, the two states with the highest Mormon populations, enforce capital punishment by firing squad, thus permitting the person's blood to be shed.

The Sin against the Holy Spirit

If you should raise the question of "blood atonement" with the missionaries, don't be misled by their possible reference to the unforgivable "sin against the Holy Spirit" referred to in Luke 12:10. The two situations are different. The sin Jesus spoke of refers to a person's final impenitence and refusal to accept God's grace. Someone who has so hardened his heart to the influence of the Holy Spirit has made himself incapable of recognizing his sinfulness and his need for mercy.

The Mormon doctrine of blood atonement, on the other hand, teaches that some sins are forgivable only if the sinner has his own blood shed in punishment. While some Mormon theologians deny that their church ever enforced such a practice, they do acknowledge that blood atonement "can only be practiced in its fulness in a day when the civil and ecclesiastical laws are administered in the same hands." Until then, Mormons must be satisfied to enact capital punishment statutes wherever they can (*MD*, 93).

Summary

The Mormon church teaches a limited, conditional atonement. Christ's saving death saves only those who are free from certain sins. Eternal life is not bestowed upon those who confess Christ and strive to live by their faith; rather, it can be earned only by diligent adherence to Mormon rules. Mormons believe that, outside literal membership in the Mormon church, there is no salvation.

Further reading: CCC 571–630; *CF*, chapter 13; *TB*, chapter 12.

5. Baptism

(*Use for Discussion 2*)

The Mormon church recognizes no baptism but its own. According to Mormons, all Christian churches are in doctrinal darkness and possess no means for bringing their members to salvation. Only Mormon baptism is valid; without it, you have no chance for eternal life.

Mormon Baptism: What It Does

Similar to Catholic baptism, Mormon baptism admits the person into communion with the church and fellowship with its members. It is also an opening up of the possibility for personal sanctification. Only validly baptized members of the Mormon church may enter into eternal life; all others are destined for lesser positions in the afterlife (see chapter 25, "Three Degrees of Glory").

No Original Sin

Mormons do not believe in an original sin committed by Adam and passed on to his descendants. Rather, they see his action of disobedience as a divinely designed necessity, one which would then permit them to become "mortal" and procreate. According to the Book of Mormon, "Adam fell that men might be; and men are, that they might have joy" (2 Nephi 2:25). The "fall," Mormons say, was a fall forward or upward. Adam is a noble hero.

Nothing in the Bible supports such an interpretation. Ask the missionaries to show, from either Old or New Testament, where God places Adam and Eve in such a dilemma. Mormon teaching says that Adam and Eve had to "transgress" the law not to eat of the tree of the knowledge of good and evil in order for them to be able to have children. Where does it say that? Mormons cannot use their own scriptures as proof of this point without begging the question.

Paul makes it clear that Adam's disobedience was a grave sin. Acting contrary to God's commandment introduced sin, suffering, and death into the world, affecting not only all men but all creation itself. The only way Adam's fall could be considered a "happy fault" (*felix culpa*) was that it meant, ultimately, that God himself would have to come among us as a man, living a full and perfect human life, being both example to and redeemer of his creation. (See Romans 5:12, 18–19 and 1 Corinthians 15:21–22.)

The "sin" Paul and all other biblical authors speak of means an offense against the goodness, sovereignty, and will of God. The "death" spoken of refers to the death of the body and the soul. Genesis 3:3 reports that God told Adam and Eve they shall not eat of the forbidden fruit, "lest ye die." We know they did not immediately die physically upon eating the fruit, but the life of grace and divine friendship was extinguished as well as binding men to eventual physical death. Therefore, Adam's act was a sin of disobedience, which led to both spiritual and physical deaths.

Mormons misunderstand the Catholic view of original sin, thinking that it involves an individual being held personally accountable for Adam's sin and consequently being personally punished for it. This is not the case. Adam alone was personally accountable for his sin, and he alone was personally punished for it. We inherit bad consequences as the result of his sin, but these are not personal punishments. The negative consequences are primarily two: (1) We are born deprived of God's sanctifying grace, and (2) We are born with a partially corrupt nature that has disordered desires (concupiscence), which lead us toward personal sin.

We have these consequences because of Adam. Like a person who was given a great fortune but squandered it and thus could not pass it on to his descendants, Adam was given God's grace of original righteousness but lost it, making him unable to pass this gift on to his children. This deprivation of righteousness/grace is what original sin is (*CCC* 417).

No Infant Baptism

Since Mormons deny that people are born deprived of sanctifying grace, they see no need to baptize infants. Rather, a child must be at least eight years old before he can be baptized into the Mormon church.

Mormons offer Book of Mormon verses depicting ancient American "prophets" harshly condemning infant baptism (Moroni 8:14). But Mormons ignore several Bible verses supporting infant baptism: Acts 16:15, 32–33 and 1 Corinthians 1:16, which reveal the apostolic practice of baptizing entire households. Nothing is said about discriminating among household members on the basis of age. The gift of the Holy Spirit, given through baptism, is specifically promised to children in Acts 2:38–39. Furthermore, baptism is the Christian equivalent of circumcision or, as Paul calls it in Colossians 2:11–12, "the circumcision of Christ."

Baptism accomplishes what outward circumcision could not —the inward, spiritual circumcision of the heart through God's grace. As the Christian equivalent of circumcision, baptism is given on similar terms. Just as if a person with the use of reason wanted to become a Jew, he had to believe in God and be circumcised, so a person with the use of reason who wants to become a Christian must believe in God and Christ and be baptized. However, just as an infant born into a Jewish family could be circumcised, though he lacked conscious, personal faith in God, so today an infant born into a Christian family can be baptized in anticipation of the faith in which he will be raised.

The testimony of the Church Fathers and other early Christian writers indicate infant baptism came from the apostles. (See *CF*, 180.)

Baptism by Immersion Only

Believing they find a biblical basis for baptism by immersion only, Mormons insist that baptism is validly performed by this method alone. It must be administered by a man holding valid Mormon priesthood and, usually, in a tank in a local Mormon meeting house.

Along with some Fundamentalist Protestants, Mormons repudiate baptism by pouring, the customary Catholic practice, though this outwardly mirrors the invisible gift of the Holy Spirit, whose giving is depicted as an act of pouring by Christ (Acts 2:17–18, 33, 10:44).

The same verses used earlier to show the probability of infant baptism also can be used to show that baptism was not always by immersion, even in apostolic times. For instance, the converted jailer of Acts 16:32–33 had brought water to the jail courtyard to bathe Paul's wounds. The same verse says he and all that were in his house were then baptized. It's unlikely there was a nearby body of water suitable for complete immersion. We may also properly infer baptism by pouring in Acts 2:41. After Peter's Pentecost sermon, "they that gladly received his word were baptized: and the same day there were added unto them about three thousand souls."

Finally, we know from the writings of the early Christians outside the New Testament that baptism was practiced by means other than immersion from the first century onward. The *Didache*, an early Christian manual of Church discipline that dates to around the year 70, states:

> In regard to baptism, baptize thus: After the foregoing instructions, baptize in the name of the Father, and of the Son, and of the Holy Spirit, in living [i.e., running] water. If you have not living [running] water, then baptize in other water; and if you are not able in cold, then in warm. If you have neither, pour water three times on the head, in the name of

the Father, and of the Son, and of the Holy Spirit [*Didache* 7:1–3].

The Who, When and How of Mormon Baptism

Candidates for Mormon baptism include children who have reached their eighth birthday, along with older converts. Potential converts are asked to commit to baptism after only the second of the hour-long discussions. Prior to baptism, the candidate is interviewed by the bishop or local congregation leader: Do you believe in the Mormon gospel? Will you support and obey the local and general authorities of the Mormon church? Will you pay a full tithe? Will you keep the Word of Wisdom? Will you observe chastity? Will you faithfully attend church meetings and fulfill whatever tasks are assigned to you?

Further reading: CCC 1213–1284; *CF*, chapter 14; *IM*, chapters 4, 13, and 23; *TB*, chapter 17.

6. Book of Mormon

(*Use for Discussion 1*)

Joseph Smith taught that the Book of Mormon "is the most correct of any book on earth, and the keystone of our religion, and a man would get nearer to God by abiding by its precepts than by any other book" [*HC* 4:461.]

Mormons will ask you to read parts of the Book of Mormon. They'll want you to pray about what you read and ask God if it truly is his word. They'll most likely give you a cheap copy of the book for free, and they hope a selective reading of its passages will lead you to acknowledge it as a true Christian book worthy of further investigation.

Mormon missionaries will also tell you that the Book of Mormon, like the Bible, has been authenticated by archaeologists, anthropologists, and historians and that moreover, the Book of Mormon was "prophesied" in the Bible and destined by God to be discovered and "brought forth" in the latter days by Smith.

The Book of Mormon—What It Is

This particular Mormon church scripture purports to be a record of ancient inhabitants of the Americas. Specifically, at the time of the Babylonian exile—early sixth century B.C.—a prophet named Lehi led some Hebrews out of Jerusalem and sailed, under God's direction, toward the New World, apparently landing somewhere in Central or South America. The sons and other descendants of Lehi broke into factions. One son, Laman, led the evil and warlike side of the family against the peaceful followers of Lehi's son Nephi.

The book traces the history of the two factions over the next 1,000 years. Prophets arose on American soil, just as in Palestine, and urged the people to repent, believe in Jesus Christ and enter his church through baptism. Shortly after his ascension, Christ visited the Americas and taught these "other sheep," instituting the sacrament of bread and wine, choosing twelve disciples, and establishing his church yet again. Peace reigned for a few years, but the old hostilities eventually returned.

Much of the book reports bloody battles between the good Nephites and the evil Lamanites. Neither a personal visit from Christ nor the secondary establishment of his church on American soil was adequate to prevent eventual spiritual apostasy and final destruction of the good Nephites. The Book of Mormon record ends in about the year 421, after a cataclysmic battle in which hundreds of thousands of men, women, and children were killed. One surviving Nephite, Moroni, had condensed the thousand years' records onto golden plates and buried them in a hill in central New York. The Book of Mormon came to be named after Moroni's father, who himself had been a prophet and great military leader.

Mormons believe God directed Smith to the burial spot near Palmyra, New York, in 1824. There, he miraculously found and translated the ancient metal plates, producing in 1830 the first version of the Book of Mormon.

The Book of Mormon—What It Isn't

It's not the "Mormon bible." Mormons accept the King James Version of the Old and New Testaments, though with reservations as to its accuracy and completeness. It's not the biography of Smith, Brigham Young or any other latter-day Mormon prophet. It's not a history of nineteenth-century Mormons and their flight from persecution. It's not authenticated by any non-Mormon research, and even many Mormon scholars question its truthfulness. Nor is it, as the Mormon church claims, the "fulness of the gospel of Jesus Christ" (D&C 20:9). Almost every uniquely Mormon belief or practice is unknown to the Book of Mormon text.

Biblical Basis for the Book of Mormon?

In order to introduce new "scripture" and new "revelation," Mormons will try to convince you that the Christian Bible itself predicts that additional testimony of Christ is needed and available. The Mormon church cites such biblical verses as the following:

> The word of the Lord came unto me, saying, Moreover, thou son of man, take thee one stick, and write upon it, For Judah, and for the children of Israel his companions: then take another stick, and write upon it, For Joseph, the stick of Ephraim, and for all the house of Israel his companions: And join them one to another into one stick; and they shall become one in thine hand [Ezek. 37:15–17].

Mormons say that Ezekiel's "sticks" refer to the Bible and the Book of Mormon. The Bible is the "stick of Judah," while the Book of Mormon is the "stick of Joseph." Joseph and his son Ephraim are the supposed ancestors of the Hebrews who fled to America in Jeremiah's time. By joining these two sticks, Mormons see the unity between traditional Christian scripture and their Book of Mormon.

Such an interpretation is impossible. The words, the context and common sense exclude such a conclusion:

A. The Hebrew word translated as "sticks" is never used in the Bible to refer to books or scrolls of any kind.

B. Even allowing that "sticks" could refer to the scrolls that were wrapped around them, the Book of Mormon was allegedly written on metal plates.

C. It was Ezekiel who wrote "For Judah" and "For Joseph." But Ezekiel did not write the whole Bible nor any part of the Book of Mormon.

D. The correct interpretation of this "acted parable" is provided in the text. Verse 22 notes that Judah (the Southern
Hebrew kingdom) and Joseph (the Northern) will be returned from exile and made one people again. Thus, the
divine message about the sticks is immediately followed
by its divine interpretation. No other explanation is permitted.

And thou shalt be brought down, and shalt speak out of the
ground, and thy speech shall be low out of the dust, and thy
voice shall be, as of one that hath a familiar spirit, out of
the ground, and thy speech shall whisper out of the dust [Is.
29:4].

The plates containing the Book of Mormon were supposedly
buried in the ground fourteen centuries before they were discovered in the mid-1820s. Therefore, Mormons say, it speaks "out
of the ground" and "low out of the dust." It has, also, a "familiar spirit" for anyone who is acquainted with the Bible, since it
"sounds" like scripture and teaches similar themes.

The prophecy is of Jerusalem's destruction and how it will be
"brought down" and humiliated for its sins. The term "whisper" means a cry of pain and fear. The same term also is used
in reference to the shrill hissings of spirit mediums and soothsay-
ers, whom the Bible calls "familiars." Mormon apologists who
use this passage apparently do not know the meaning of the term
"familiar spirit," which indicates a spirit used by a medium as a
regular guide to the spirit world.

And the vision of all is become unto you as the words of a
book that is sealed, which men deliver to one that is learned,
saying, Read this, I pray thee: and he saith, I cannot; for it is
sealed: And the book is delivered to him that is not learned,
saying, Read this, I pray thee: and he saith, I am not learned
[Is. 29:11–12].

This passage speaks of the people of Judah's failure to com-
prehend that God was going to deliver them. They refused to

understand the prophecy he gave of this, just as a literate person cannot read a scroll that's sealed shut and an illiterate person cannot read anything.

Mormons misapply this passage to suit their beliefs. At one point, Smith copied a few characters from the golden plates and sent them to a Columbia college professor. This scholar, Professor Anthon, is said to have authenticated the writing, which has become known as "reformed Egyptian," and its translation. When Anthon asked to see the complete book, he was told that it was sealed. In reply, he said, "I cannot read a sealed book." In this, Mormons say, he fulfilled Isaiah 29:11–12.

Anthon later denied that he verified the sample writing. There have never been any other examples of such a language, so he could not have approved the English "translation" of it. (As you might expect, the metal plates on which the Book of Mormon was first written were "miraculously" taken back to heaven, prohibiting any objective verification.)

Mormons pride themselves in taking the Bible "literally." Yet here, as in the previous passages, a literal interpretation cannot support their use of these verses. Anthon allegedly read the sample text and pronounced its translation correct. Yet Isaiah said the learned man could not read it. Isaiah also noted the book went first to the learned man and later to the unlearned. But Smith originated the manuscript that Anthon "read." In neither case do we hear anything about a translation.

This is the third time I am coming to you. In the mouth of two or three witnesses shall every word be established [2 Cor. 13:1].

In 1981, attempting to cultivate a Christian persona, the Mormon church added to its Book of Mormon the subtitle: "Another Testament of Jesus Christ." Mormons claim that the Book of Mormon is another witness to Jesus' divinity and mission. Thus it fulfills the paradigm of a truth that shall be established by two or three witnesses.

This principle was originally a regulation in the law courts of ancient Israel to prevent people from being put to death based on the testimony of only one witness (Deut. 17:5). In 2 Corinthians, Paul makes a spiritual application of it, speaking of how he is about to visit their church for the third time and testify to them regarding the truth.

"Translating" the Golden Plates

Smith, after supposedly being led by an angel to the plates' burial place, said he was able to translate the "reformed Egyptian" on the plates "by the gift and power of God." He would never reveal the specifics of this process. Observers produced various scenarios. Most, however, agree that Smith made use of a "seer stone"—a smooth rock that he placed in his hat. Smith would then bury his face in the hat and the "translation" of the ancient writings would appear on the stone. He then dictated it to a scribe who wrote the English and repeated it to Smith, who verified it. At that point, new words appeared on the stone and the translation of the long document (over 500 pages) proceeded. Smith didn't really make use of the plates at all. Sometimes they were not even in the room when he "translated" them. In fact, nobody apparently ever saw the plates.

Witnesses of the Book of Mormon?

The Book of Mormon contains statements by two groups of witnesses. "The Testimony of Three Witnesses" was made by Oliver Cowdery, an early collaborator with Smith; David Whitmer, Cowdery's brother-in-law; and Martin Harris, who financed the book's first printing. According to their testimony, they were "shown" the gold plates by an angel "by the power of God." In other words, they had a "spiritual vision" of the plates. All three men left or were excommunicated from the Mormon church.

Smith subsequently vilified their characters, calling them "wicked," "dumb ass" and "too mean to mention; and we had liked to have forgotten them" (D&C 3:12; *HC* 3:228, 231–232).

Mormons maintain that none of the witnesses ever recanted his testimony about the Book of Mormon. There is, however, some indication that Cowdery did. As for the others, Whitmer led a church that accepted the Book of Mormon but repudiated Smith and many of his other "prophetic" revelations. Harris gave equal testimony to the Shakers' sacred records.

The Book of Mormon and Smith said there were to be only these three witnesses. However, God changed his mind and had Smith seek a statement from eight other men. These included his father and two brothers, and four brothers and a brother-in-law of Whitmer.

The Mormon church doesn't tell you that the eight men were not present at the same time to "see" the plates. Only one asserted he "handled" the plates, and then only "by a supernatural power" (*HC* 3:307). William, another Smith brother, stated that whatever any of these witnesses may have "hefted" was wrapped in a sack. Hiram Page, one of these eight, later produced his own "seer stone" and made prophecies backed by Cowdery and Whitmer. Three more of the eight left or were excommunicated from the Mormon church.

At best, what you have is eleven men who claim to have had a "vision" of the plates. Though the Mormon church today portrays them as witnesses of sterling character and honest report, Smith did not share that view. Most of them at various times were thrown out of his church or left in disgust.

The Book of Mormon Isn't Christian

If you like bloody, detailed accounts of wars and intrigues, you'll get more than your fill in the Book of Mormon. If you don't mind reading seventy words when five or ten would do, go ahead. If you think that because the book is divided into chapters and verses and uses antiquated vocabulary, it's valid scripture, read on.

While much of the book is inoffensive, theologically, it's unorthodox because it frequently confuses the persons of God, wavering between belief in just one divine person (modalism) and two persons (binitarianism). The "sacrament" of bread and wine is presented as merely a symbolic memorial and infant baptism is condemned. Although some branches of Protestantism may agree with parts of this, Catholics easily recognize that such teachings contradict the Old and New Testaments and the historic creeds.

The Book of Mormon Isn't Mormon

Missionaries use the book as a conversion tool. By reading specially selected passages, especially those dealing with Jesus Christ's visit to the Hebrew Nephites in the New World (3 Nephi), you are expected to see the beauty of the text and accept as authentic the church and missionaries who promote it. Once you bite this bait, you are going to be reeled in and asked to accept real Mormon beliefs and practices. These are not found in the Book of Mormon and developed only gradually, after the Book of Mormon was completed. Not found in the book claimed to be the "most correct" of any book and the "fulness of the gospel" are such fundamental Mormon beliefs as:

1. God was once a mortal man on another planet.

2. God the Father has a glorified, physical body of flesh and bones.

3. Each soul has existed from eternity and had a "spirit birth" ages before it was placed in a human body.

4. Faithful Mormon men may become gods and rule over kingdoms as God the Father rules this one.

5. There are, therefore, many gods.

6. Attendance at Mormon temple rituals is essential for salvation.

7. Refraining from coffee, tea, alcohol, and tobacco is essential for salvation.

8. Paying a full tithe is essential for salvation.

The Book of Mormon mentions none of this. You have to be led into these "deeper" truths gradually. If you let the fairly bland Book of Mormon hook you, there's no telling how deeply you'll be burned by real Mormonism.

Problems with the Book of Mormon

Aside from the theological problems noted above, the book presents its defenders with insurmountable problems.

1. GEOGRAPHY AND ARCHAEOLOGY

Ask the missionaries to show you a map of the American area where the book's events took place. They won't be able to. There are no maps in the Book of Mormon, since even Mormon scholars can't agree on the locations. By contrast, the Bible *is* accompanied by verifiable maps for nearly all its significant events. Independent research has located the important cities and many other features mentioned in the Old and New Testaments. Even Mormon general authorities contradict one another about the extent of the Nephite civilization. The older view was that it spread over most of North and Central America. The current opinion, considered easier to defend, is that it covered only a limited territory in Central America, though even that area does not show evidence of the civilization Mormon apologists claim it to have held.

The Book of Mormon maintains that the Nephites had developed a vast system of roads and cities, together with advanced metallurgy and cloth production. No evidence has been found to back this assertion. It also talks about elephants, horses, cows, silk, and olive trees. None of these existed in America at any time during the supposed 1000-year history of the Nephite civilization. Most were introduced only centuries later, after the coming of Europeans.

Sometimes a zealous missionary will tell you the Book of Mormon has been authenticated by one prestigious organization or another, such as the Smithsonian Institute or the National Geographic Society. It hasn't. Ask to see their proof. In return, show them the following, which are taken from the standard replies sent by the Smithsonian and National Geographic Society in response to inquiries by those who have heard inaccurate Mormon claims:

a. "The Smithsonian Institution has never used the Book of Mormon in any way as a scientific guide. Smithsonian archaeologists see no direct correlation between the archaeology of the New World and the subject matter of the book."

b. ". . . [N]either the Society nor any other institution of equal prestige has ever used the Book of Mormon in locating archaeological sites. Although many Mormon sources claim that the Book of Mormon has been substantiated by archaeological findings, this claim has not been substantiated."

2. LANGUAGE

The Book of Mormon was supposedly written in "reformed Egyptian," but what is that? If the Nephite civilization, widespread and active for a millennium in the New World, used such a language, why do we have no remnants of it? If it were a "sacred language" reserved only to the writing of scripture, where is any evidence of their daily Hebrew? None has been found. Furthermore, why would devout Jews use the hated language of their Egyptian oppressors in writing holy books, anyway?

Second, if Lehi left Jerusalem in 600 B.C. and brought with him only the writings of the Jewish prophets to that time, why are there sizable plagiarisms from the New Testament in the Book of Mormon? (Compare, for example, Alma 19 with John 11, 1 Nephi 18 with Mark 4, Ether 8:10–12 with Matt. 14:6–11; see also Hugh Nibley, *Since Cumorah*, 127 and Jerald and Sandra Tanner's *The Case Against Mormonism*, 2:86–87.)

Third, large portions of the book of Isaiah are duplicated in the Book of Mormon. Each biblical reference, including whole chapters lifted from the Old or New Testament, is given in the King James version, a translation made over a thousand years after the last Nephite prophet, but available to Smith (see especially 2 Nephi 7–8, 12–24).

Fourth, the Book of Mormon uses several Greek (and even French!) terms. These languages would have been unknown to the Hebrew-American immigrants (see 3 Nephi 9:18, 19:4, 6:19, Jacob 7:27).

Fifth, many Old Testament observances are omitted in the book. Nothing is said of Passover, for example. We'd expect so central a feast to at least be mentioned by the "American" Hebrews.

Sixth, you learn nothing new about Jesus Christ from the Book of Mormon. His teachings mirror those already presented in the New Testament.

Finally, though the book is said to have been translated by the power of God, it has gone through numerous revisions. Over 4,000 changes have been made—most for grammar, spelling or punctuation, but some for doctrinal purposes. If the book's translation had received the Lord's approval, why make such changes?

Well, Should I Read It or Not?

Eager missionaries will offer you a copy of the book and ask you to read portions of it prayerfully. They cite a passage from the last book of the Book of Mormon:

Behold, I would exhort you that when ye shall read these things, if it be wisdom in God that ye should read them . . . that ye shall receive these things, and ponder it in your hearts. . . . I would exhort you that ye would ask God, the Eternal Father, in the name of Christ, if these things are not true; and if ye shall ask with a sincere heart, with real intent, having faith in Christ, he will manifest the truth of it unto you, by the power of the Holy Ghost [Moroni 10:3–4].

The deck is stacked. If you're sincere and have faith, you'll conclude the Book of Mormon is true. If you get a sign (Mormons sometimes call it a "burning in the bosom"), how can you contradict it? After all, God has blessed you with this inner conviction. You won't permit anything contrary to shake your new "faith." Logic and contrary evidence notwithstanding, you've got yourself a "testimony"! It's on such subjective feelings that Mormonism builds its elaborate system of confusing and contradictory beliefs.

As further incentive, Mormons will quote James 1:5:

If any of you lack wisdom, let him ask of God, that giveth to all men liberally, and upbraideth not; and it shall be given him.

They think this blesses their practice of seeking the truth by praying about it. It doesn't.

If I am trying to find something out, I may pray that God will lead me to the evidence I need, but I don't demand that he give me a direct, personal revelation. That is not his typical pattern, and it is the sin of presumption to act as if it is. If I need to know the truth about something, I study it, research it, investigate it. If I've already been shown the truth, it is presumption at best to continue to pray to know it, though I may and must pray to be able to accept and live it. Bottom line, I do not ask God to tell me whether *his* word is true.

The Book of Mormon denies basic Catholic truths, contradicts the archaeological record and is unsupported by objective evidence. No amount of prayer will change that, and you put yourself in grave spiritual jeopardy if you cut loose the ties with objective evidence and pray for a "burning in the bosom."

However, since Mormons accept the principle of individual private revelation concerning whether a book is of God, it is fair to ask them to apply their own principle. Ask the Mormon to read the *Catechism of the Catholic Church*. Offer to guide him in his reading. See how far you get.

B. H. Roberts, Mormon General Authority, on Book of Mormon Authorship:

[W]as Joseph Smith possessed of a sufficiently vivid and creative imagination as to produce such a work as the Book of Mormon from . . . such common knowledge as was extant in communities where he lived in his boyhood and young manhood . . . ? That such power of imagination would have to be of a high order is conceded; that Joseph Smith possessed such a gift of mind there can be no question [*Studies of the Book of Mormon*, 243].

Further reading: CCC 101–141; *IM*, chapters 29–31.

7. Chastity and Sexual Morality

(*Use for Discussion 4*)

Mormons cultivate an image of wholesome, happy families. Individual members are expected to live celibately before marriage and then faithfully to their lawful spouse. Are such standards any different from those of the Catholic Church? Not at all!

> Know ye not that ye are the temple of God, and that the Spirit of God dwelleth in you? [1 Cor. 3:16].

Catholics have always answered Paul's question with an unqualified *Yes*. Every moral teaching of the New Testament finds sincere acceptance by the Church and its faithful members. Mormons do not corner the market, nor even lead the pack, in the area of sexual morality.

But in fact, the Mormon church doesn't really practice what it preaches. I'm not saying this because many, or even a few, of its members fail to live up to its expectations. That's the case in any religious group. An individual's lapses can't be held against the institution. What I'm saying is that the Mormon church presents itself as pro-family and pro-life, while permitting abortion, artificial contraception, and divorce followed by remarriage. As with so many of its doctrines and practices, the Mormon church's current position on these issues contradicts former beliefs.

Abortion

Compare the church's statement in its 1988 handbook, *Gospel Principles*, with that of the 1992 edition:

1988 edition: There is no excuse for abortion unless the life of the mother is seriously threatened [241].

1992 edition: There is seldom any excuse for abortion. The only exceptions are when—1. Pregnancy has resulted from incest or rape. 2. The life or health of the woman is in jeopardy in the opinion of competent medical authority; or 3. The fetus is known, by competent medical authority, to have severe defects that will not allow the baby to survive beyond birth [251].

Prior to the 1992 printing, the Mormon church permitted abortion if the mother's life were seriously threatened. While appearing stringent, this is a pro-abortion stand. It permitted the killing of the innocent unborn child to "save" the life of the mother—a situation that medical science has rendered virtually nonexistent and which sound moral theology has always rejected as "doing evil that good may come."

The more recent Mormon position is of course the "politically correct" one. Since church policy is determined by divine revelation, apparently God has loosened his law.

Ask your Mormon acquaintances about a "fetus." Chances are, they'll quote (correctly) leaders' statements referring to the unborn "child" and innocent "human baby." Then ask them about their church's position on abortion. They'll probably say, "We're pro-life," or "Only in the case of the mother's life." Then point out the true Mormon position and ask them to justify it. How can the church be so "pro-life" yet permit the killing of an "innocent child" in so many cases?

Artificial Contraception

The same is true for artificial contraception. Though various Mormon prophets have urged couples to avoid it, unnatural birth control is left up to the individuals' conscience. You can contracept and still remain a temple-worthy member. See "Birth Control," *EM* vol. 1.

Divorce and Remarriage

Though Christ forbids remarriage after divorce, calling it adultery (Mark 10:10–11), the Mormon church permits it. While its motto is "Families forever," many of its families don't make it through this lifetime, to say nothing of the eternities.

Mormons may divorce and remarry and remain in good standing. Couples who participate in a temple ceremony to seal their marriage for eternity can even have their sealings "canceled" (effectively, a celestial divorce). This would then permit a subsequent "eternal" marriage inside the temple to the next spouse. Statistics show that divorced Mormons are more likely than divorced non-Mormons to remarry. Three-fourths of divorced Mormons remarry ("Divorce," *EM*, vol. 1). Despite the Mormon emphasis on family, Utah, which is 70 percent Mormon, actually has a divorce rate slightly higher than the U.S. average (4.7 divorces per thousand persons per year versus 4.6 nationally, according to *The American Almanac 1996–1997*, 107).

Euthanasia

The killing of the elderly, weak, sick, or unwanted is not directly related to sexual morality. It is, however, related to the cavalier attitude we see toward the unwanted unborn. President Gordon B. Hinckley, the current prophet, made a comment in 1997 that has produced a whirlwind of discussion. You might alert the missionary to be prepared to defend a possible shift in yet another church teaching. In an interview, Hinckley said,

> With reference to euthanasia, no, at this point at least, we haven't favored that [San Francisco *Chronicle*, April 13, 1997, 3/Z1].

Can you imagine any biblical prophet vacillating on so important an issue? Is Hinckley waiting for God to reveal to him the correct position? Or is he hinting that the door may be opened to such murders in the future? If so, he implies that the door is now ajar, and those Mormons looking for a pretext to slip through may find one in his words.

There is something odd about an institution that is certain God forbids a cup of coffee or a glass of wine but can't make up his mind about killing babies or the elderly.

Further reading: CCC 2270–2275 (abortion), 2276–2279 (euthanasia), 2331–2365, 2380–2381, 2387–2400 (chastity), 2366–2379 (contraception), 2382–2386 (divorce); *IM,* chapter 8.

8. The Church

(*Use for Discussion 3*)

According to Mormon apostle Bruce R. McConkie,

> One of the great and eternal verities that all men are required by their Creator to accept without reservation is that there is only one true church. How can churches that teach conflicting doctrines and perform differing ordinances all be true? Are we wrong in saying that truth is truth, and one truth is always in perfect harmony with every other truth? [*A New Witness for the Articles of Faith*, 338].

Catholics agree with every word of this statement. Christ instituted one Church, which he commissioned to teach eternal truth. Groups that teach contrary doctrines have departed from full union with him. The dispute is over which church is Christ's. Catholics can simply point to the historical record: The Catholic Church *was* founded by Jesus two thousand years ago. This is a matter of objective history. However, Mormons declare that all Christian churches—the Catholic Church included—are in apostasy and that theirs alone is Christ's true church.

The Mormon Church—Named after Christ

"How can you not think we're Christians? Even our title— The Church of Jesus Christ of Latter-day Saints—bears the name of Jesus Christ."

Yes, it does—*now*. But in the first few years of its existence, the Mormon church had several names, all supposedly given to it by revelation, before it settled on its current title. But names prove nothing. Anyone can name their church anything they want, and a quick glance at a list of past or present Protestant churches, as well as quasi-Christian sects, will show you that many of them use the name of Jesus Christ in their title.

The Mormon Church—Organized Exactly Like the New Testament Church?

According to Mormon theologians, today's true church must be organized after the pattern of the early church. They point, for example, to Ephesians 2:19-20:

> Now therefore ye are no more strangers and foreigners, but fellow-citizens with the saints, and of the household of God; And are built upon the foundation of the apostles and prophets, Jesus Christ himself being the chief corner stone.

"You see," Mormons say, "the Lord's church has to have apostles and prophets. We have them. Where are yours?"

Don't be fooled by this word game. You can assign any title you like to your leaders. As with the name of the church, the mere titles of "prophets" and "apostles" do not make it so.

Look at the Ephesians passage carefully. The true Church has *already* been built on the foundation of apostles and prophets. Just as there is but one corner stone, Jesus Christ, there is but one foundation, God's prophets and the Lord's twelve apostles.

The Mormon church claims to restore not only lost teachings but the true structure of Christ's church as he established it two thousand years ago in Palestine. Other topics in this book deal with the so-called restored doctrines. At this point, let's see how closely Mormon church organization mirrors that of the early Church.

1. *The First Presidency* includes the President of the Church and his two counselors. They are "prophets, seers, and revelators" to the whole church. Usually, the two counselors are chosen from the ranks of the apostles. There is no mention of a "First Presidency" (or, for that matter, *any* "presidency") in the New Testament.

2. *The Quorum of the Twelve Apostles* are men chosen from the fields of business, education, law and other professions. Though there are always twelve who hold this position, the two serving in the First Presidency raise the number to fourteen. These men are appointed for life. They and the First Presidency receive incomes from church tithes.

In the New Testament, the twelve was a select group of apostles who had witnessed Jesus' earthly ministry. This was the key qualification for an apostle to be a member of the New Testament twelve (Acts 1:21–22). No member of the Mormon Quorum of Twelve meets this test. Mormons consequently mistake the purpose of the twelve, which was to serve as a link between Jesus' earthly ministry and later Church history; it was not meant to be a perpetual body.

3. *The Quorums of the Seventies:* Jesus appointed seventy men (Luke 10:1) as additional preachers of the gospel for a particular preaching mission during his earthly ministry and sent them throughout the land to bear witness. Mormons currently have several quorums of Seventies, none of which actually contains seventy men. They are variously appointed to five-year terms or for "life," with a mandatory retirement age. They also receive payment from the Mormon church.

The above three groups are termed the "General Authorities" of the church. Other offices include area and regional authorities, none of which are found in the New Testament.

4. "Local authorities" refer to *stake presidents* and ward bishops. A stake is a geographical unit of the church usually comprising about 2,000 members. It is directed by a president with his two counselors. They are called "President." There is no mention of stake presidencies in the New Testament or any other writing of the apostolic era. "Stakes" also were not divisions in the New Testament Church.

5. The lowest level of church hierarchy is the *ward bishopric*, comprised of a bishop and his two counselors. These men are responsible for the spiritual and temporal affairs of their ward, a unit comprised of about 200 households. Those who serve in stake and ward positions do not currently receive a church income and must support themselves and their families by secular jobs. "Wards" were not divisions in the New Testament Church.

In no way, therefore, do we see the organizational structure of the Mormon church corresponding to that of the New Testament Church. Mormons may have pinched a few titles mentioned in the New Testament, but that does not mean its structure mirrors that used in the New Testament.

Organizational units have been added to and removed from the Mormon church since its beginning in 1830. Offices and titles have changed frequently. There is no indication that the church has finally settled upon one hierarchical format. In any case, it is, in its present form, far removed from the pattern presented by the New Testament church. Mormon structure, like the doctrines it says it has restored, finds no basis in the preaching and practice of the original—and only—apostles.

The Mormon Church Has Its Share of Apostates

Mormon leaders claim that the hundreds of sects within historical Christianity are proof that the true Church fell into apostasy after

Jesus' apostles died. In its 170-year history, the Mormon church itself has been wracked by conflict and division. The following are just some of the splinter groups arising from the Mormon movement:

Aaronic Order, Church of Jesus Christ, Church of the First Born, Church of Jesus Christ of Saints of the Most High, Kingdom of Heaven, Mormon Scripture Researchers, Zion's Order, Inc., Apostolic United Brethren, Christ's Church, Church of Jesus Christ of the Saints in Zion, Church of the First Born of the Fullness of Times, Confederate Nations of Israel, Church of the Lamb of God, Church of the New Covenant in Christ, Millennial Church of Jesus Christ, Perfected Church of Jesus Christ Immaculate Latter-Day Saints, Sons Ahman Israel, United Order Effort, Center Branch of the Lord's Remnant, Church of Christ (Temple Lot), Church of Christ Immanuel, Church of Jesus Christ (Protest Movement), Church of Jesus Christ Restored, Reorganized Church of Jesus Christ of Latter Day Saints, True Church of Jesus Christ Restored [*The Encyclopedia of American Religions*, vol. II, 187–210].

Further reading: CCC 172–175, 748–913; *CF*, chapters 17 and 18; *TB*, chapter 13 and 14; *IM*, chapter 3.

9. Continuous Revelation

(*Use for Discussion 6*)

We believe all that God has revealed, all that He does now reveal, and we believe that He will yet reveal many great and important things pertaining to the Kingdom of God [Articles of Faith, 9].

If you've worked your way to Discussion 6, and if you've also studied this manual, you'll see that Mormon teachings on a variety of subjects are often confusing and at times downright contradictory. This is partly because of the Mormon notion of "continuous revelation." Mormons believe that their God, who is an eternally changeable deity, may give changing commands to his followers.

Mormons are told that the proper attitude toward this divine fluctuation is not adherence or even attention to the previous teachings of even Mormon prophets and scriptures but obedience to current edicts.

"Fourteen Fundamentals in Following the Prophets"

In 1980, a few years before becoming President and Prophet of the Mormon church, Ezra Taft Benson addressed the students at Brigham Young University. The young people would be crowned with God's glory if they observe his "fourteen fundamentals." He told them the Mormon prophet is the only man who speaks for the Lord in everything, not just religious matters. In this, he is not required to have any earthly training whatsoever since he enjoys direct divine revelation on any topic. The only way to blessing is to follow the prophet unreservedly, since he will never lead the church astray.

Two of Benson's points in particular touched on the subject of "continuous revelation."

1. The living prophet is more important than the scriptures. Benson cited Brigham Young, an early Mormon prophet, who exclaimed, "[W]hen compared with the living oracles those books [the Bible and Mormon scriptures] are nothing to me; those books do not convey the word of God direct to us now, as do the words of a Prophet" [as recorded by President Wilford Woodruff; *Conference Reports*, Oct. 1897, 18–19].

2. The living prophet is more important than a dead prophet. In other words, should the teachings of the current Mormon leadership contradict that of previous prophets, don't be baffled or alarmed. Simply ignore what was taught before and adhere now to the latest decree. In his "Fourteen Fundamentals in Following the Prophets" speech, Benson concludes, "Beware of those who would pit the dead prophets against the living prophets, for the living prophets always take precedence" [ibid. 3–5].

"Abandon All Logic, Ye Who Enter Here"?

Polygamy was once taught as a requirement for eternal salvation. Those who now practice it are excommunicated. At one time, God forbade black people to hold the Mormon priesthood at least until Christ's Second Coming. In 1978, God changed his mind. Those who denied the change are also excommunicated. Abortion was once condemned and strictly limited. The current, though largely unadvertised, policy of the church is permissive. Young once taught Adam was the God of this world. After denying for years that he ever said it, contemporary Mormon scholars admit he taught it but was nonetheless wrong. Smith's earliest writings, including the Book of Mormon, proclaimed only one God. Mormons now believe in innumerable gods.

If your God is changeable, then I guess he's entitled to change his mind. Again and again. But if you believe in the infinite and unchanging God revealed in Scripture (Mal. 3:6; Jas. 1:17), you know that he once for all revealed the fullness of his word in his Son (Heb. 1:1-2), who himself established one Church that would remain faithful forever and teach all nations in all times (Matt. 28:19-20).

Further reading: CCC 65-100; *IM,* chapter 33.

10. Families

(*Use for Discussion 4*)

The Mormon slogan "Families can be forever" means that, unlike all other married couples, who are married "till death do them part," the faithful Mormon couple and their children can live as one for all eternity.

If you marry your mate in a Mormon temple, in a ceremony called "sealing," you are married, says the church, for time and all eternity. Even if you are widowed and take another spouse, you are sealed forever to your first. At the resurrection of the dead, the husband will call his wife to his side. They and their children will then progress to greater and greater glory, climaxing in their own divinization. They will then rule over their own world and populate it with their billions of new spirit children.

Mormons seem to think that only they can assure you of a reunion with your loved ones in heaven. This is one reason why you often see Mormons go into action at the death of a non-member's spouse, parent or child. If your spouse died, they would tell you how you could still save your marriage by becoming Mormon and having ordinances done by proxy for the deceased. The same holds for any deceased loved one.

But ask the missionaries,

"Your church holds out the promise that my spouse and children can be with me for all eternity, right?"

"Right."

"Well, suppose I live a faithful Mormon life, but my spouse is less devoted. Suppose, too, that of our six children, two live righteously, two are only casual Latter-day Saints, and two completely abandon the church. Will we still be together?"

If the missionaries know enough of their church's teachings, and if they don't dodge the question, they'll have to tell you, "No, sorry. That won't work. You see, heaven consists of several compartments. Depending on your membership status and personal devotedness, you will be assigned to one of those levels. The way you've described it, your family will probably be spread out over three different compartments. Those in the higher categories can briefly visit those below them, but not vice versa. Only those members who make it to the highest level will remain in a family unit forever."

How "forever" is that? Though Mormonism teaches virtually everyone will attain some level of heavenly happiness (another reason for its appeal), very few of even its own members could achieve the highest level where families are permitted to stay together. Everyone else is scattered throughout the other eternal "degrees."

A Catholic Response

Jesus explicitly taught that marriages *do not* continue into the next life:

> The children of this world marry, and are given in marriage: But they which shall be accounted worthy to obtain that world, and the resurrection from the dead, neither marry, nor are given in marriage: Neither can they die any more: for they are equal unto the angels; and are the children of God, being the children of the resurrection [Luke 20:34–36].

Jesus does not make exceptions for anybody. The class of the saved will not be married since the primary function of marriage —the procreation of the human race—will no longer be needed. For Mormons who deny Jesus' plain words, we can only answer as the Lord himself did on this occasion:

> Ye do err, not knowing the scriptures, nor the power of God [Matt. 22:30; part of Matthew's parallel to Luke 20:34–36].

The idea that people will be living separate, anonymous eternities is wrong. The Catholic faith has always taught that the saved in heaven rejoice forever in perfect love and communion. Scripture abounds with references to heaven as a city, a kingdom, a banquet. Each of these images indicates community. Our bodies and our souls will be perfected and reunited. So, too, our relationships. We will know and be known, love and be loved. Though our hearts will be open to all, there will be a special bond between family members and friends.

The Mormon church actually gives families *less* assurance of being together in the afterlife since it compartmentalizes the afterlife of the righteous into different units, from which family members can have only limited, occasional visits with members in other units.

Polygamy—a Brief Aside

For about 45 years, until 1890, the Mormon church taught its members to live the principle of "plural marriage." A man financially able was to take more than one wife and raise up children from them. This was in direct obedience to a supposed revelation from God that Smith claimed he received in the 1830s. Smith himself practiced polygamy secretly for several years, while publicly denying it, before he made the doctrine public.

In the summer of 1835, it was rumored that Smith had taken to himself a teenaged girl who had been staying in the Smith home. Fanny Alger has been listed as the first of Smith's polygamous wives, a young lady who, when she was no longer able "to conceal the consequences of her celestial [i.e., carnal] relation with the prophet," was driven out by Smith's furious first wife, Emma (see Linda King Newell and Valeen Tippetts Avery, *Mormon Enigma: Emma Hale Smith*, 65–67).

Over the next seven years, Smith is said to have added a dozen "wives," sealed to him with or without Emma's knowledge (Andrew Jenson, *Historical Record*, 6:233–234). There is also evidence that Smith also asked for and received the lawful wives of other living men. Mormon President Jedediah M. Grant once recalled, "What would a man of God say, who felt aright, when Joseph . . . came and said, 'I want your wife'? 'O yes,' he would say, 'here she is, there are plenty more' " (*Journal of Discourses* 2:14).

The mandate for polygamy was first "revealed" by God on July 12, 1843, but was not formally announced until 1852. The revelation was canonized as Doctrine and Covenants 132 in 1876 and voted on by the general membership in 1880. (Mormons hold *pro forma* votes on whether a revelation is of God or not.) God Almighty supposedly states, in D&C 132:2, that "all those who have this law revealed unto them must obey the same." No one can reject this "new and everlasting covenant" and enter into heavenly glory (verse 3). Permission is granted for a man to marry more than one wife (verses 44, 48, 61, 62). Also in D&C 132, Smith's first wife, Emma, is commanded by Christ to accept all the wives Smith already had taken, even if surreptitiously, or suffer destruction (verses 52, 54). Verse 61 requires that the first wife give permission for the husband to take additional wives.

Still, this "revelation" came in 1843, almost a decade after Smith first began living as a polygamist. How could this be explained? When confronted with the dilemma of an adulterous prophet or one who simply implemented the official church policy of polygamy years earlier than the rest of the membership, Mormon officials opted for the latter. According to the current official heading for D&C 132, the principles and doctrines involved in this 1843 dictum "had been known by the Prophet since 1831," four years before the Alger affair. Though this explanation allowed Smith to save face, there was at least one principle of the revelation he didn't seem to know. He knew enough to take more wives, but didn't know enough to ask Emma's permission.

Of course, the 1843 polygamy "revelation" lacks all credibility, coming years after Smith had been acquiring polygamous unions. Smith introduced it to justify his previous behavior.

Federal legislation against polygamy and prosecution of polygamists, together with Utah's drive for statehood, led later Mormon prophet Wilford Woodruff to ban the practice in 1890. He said he was told to do so by the same God who had earlier commanded it as an "everlasting covenant." Yet another example of Mormonism's continually reversing "continuous revelation."

Though currently banned by the Mormon church, polygamy is still practiced in the Western U.S. by tens of thousands who refuse to go along with the new regulations. Though the Mormon church now excommunicates known polygamists, it prophesies that in the future polygamy will again be permitted and practiced and that polygamy is the rule for those in the celestial kingdom.

Further reading: CCC 1023–1029, 1042–1050, 1655–1658, 2201–2233; *IM*, chapters 8, 24, and 26.

11. First Vision

(*Use for Discussion 1*)

The greatest event that has ever occurred in the world, since the resurrection of the Son of God from the tomb and his ascension on high, was the coming of the Father and of the Son to that boy Joseph Smith [Joseph F. Smith, *Gospel Doctrine*, 495].

Prospective converts must be taught the current version of Smith's vision. It's an essential part of the first discussion, and those who would be baptized into the Mormon church must accept it.

Contents of the "First Vision"—
the Current Mormon Version

The missionaries might direct you to a Mormon scripture entitled Joseph Smith—History, a part of a longer work called the Pearl of Great Price. In this account, Smith reports a vision of the Father and the Son, saying that when he was fourteen, a great religious revival took place in the Palmyra district of central New York. This was in the year 1820. Having been raised in a "spiritual but not religious" family, Smith was anxious to know which of the competing Protestant sects was true. To this purpose, he read James 1:5 and sought the Lord's advice in prayer. Retiring to a grove, he was given a vision of the physical bodies of the Father and Jesus. The Father introduced his Son, who told Smith that he "must join none of" the churches, "for they are all wrong . . . all their creeds were an abomination" in the sight of God, and those who professed the traditional Christian faith "were all corrupt."

Two Fatal Heresies

The First Vision implies that Christianity disappeared from the earth centuries ago. The gates of hell had indeed prevailed against the true Church, which would be restored only by the boy-prophet. In the intervening generations, those who worshipped the Lord in the Catholic, Orthodox, and Protestant churches drew near to him with their lips, but their hearts were far from him. All priestly authority and valid ordinances (sacraments) had vanished from among men, leaving them with no access to grace nor means of salvation. This is a heresy, for it directly contradicts Christ's promises: "I will build my church; and the gates of hell shall not prevail against it" (Matt. 16:18b) and "[L]o, I am with you alway[s], even unto the end of the world" (Matt. 28:20).

A second heresy supposedly revealed in the First Vision deals with the Godhead. According to the final version of the Vision, Smith saw the flesh-and-bones bodies of the Father and the Son. Christianity has constantly maintained that Jesus, fully God and fully man, was physically raised from the dead (anticipating the general resurrection, in which all humans will receive their physical bodies again) and that he ascended to heaven with his human body. There is no dispute with Mormonism on this point. But Christianity also teaches that God the Father (as well as God the Holy Spirit) is a Spirit, without material parts. Otherwise, he could not be infinite, unbounded and all-present. For the Mormon church to teach that God the Father has a material body flies in the face of reason and the universal faith. It also denies Christ's statements: "God *is* a Spirit" (John 4:23a) and "a spirit hath not flesh and bones" (Luke 24:39b).

Mormonism Stands or Falls on the First Vision

Mormon President Spencer W. Kimball asserted that "Joseph Smith's First Vision restored knowledge of God. Of all the great events of the century, none compared with the First Vision of Joseph Smith" (*The Teachings of Spencer W. Kimball*, 428).

A thorough treatment of the problems of the official version of the First Vision is found in *Inside Mormonism: What Mormons Really Believe* (San Diego: Catholic Answers, 1999), chapter 28. I summarize here:

1. There was no revival in 1820. The nearest possible date is 1824–1825, when Smith would no longer be an innocent youth.

2. Though Smith maintained that his report of the vision was met with general disbelief and widespread personal persecution, there is not a single account of such activities in any newspaper of the time. Note that these publications, in later years, reveled in reporting anything that would embarrass the new sect.

3. The present, printed version dates from Smith's writings in 1838 and was printed publicly four years later. Thus, his account was put into general circulation over twenty years after it supposedly took place.

4. In those intervening years, Smith had given conflicting versions of this vision. In 1832, he proclaimed that the Lord (Jesus Christ) had appeared to him, with no mention of the Father. In 1835, he wrote that two unnamed persons had appeared to him in the midst of flame, together with many angels. No mention is made of God.

5. In 1835, Smith gave for publication a story of his first alleged supernatural encounter. According to this story, the religious revival took place in 1823, Smith did not retire to the woods, did not see God the Father or God the Son, and was simply visited by an angel in his bedroom. Either Smith was deliberately suppressing the story of the First Vision (the earliest version of which he wrote in his own hand in 1832), and thus misleading his flock concerning

the origin of their faith, or, due to the many different stories he had told about his alleged supernatural encounters and how they started, the vision in the grove story simply slipped his mind.

6. Due to the late date of the First Vision story and the lofty claims it makes (being given the message by both God the Father and Jesus Christ), the story appears to be a late creation intended to bolster Smith's authority. It seems to have been one of a number of different stories concerning how Smith first had contact with the supernatural, and after it went through several versions, it was eventually integrated with the angel stories to form the current Mormon picture of how Smith became a seer.

7. Still, there was significant confusion over the matter, even at the time. Smith's immediate successors as Mormon prophets, Brigham Young and John Taylor, stated only that Smith had been visited by an angel.

President Hugh B. Brown on the First Vision:

The first vision of the Prophet Joseph Smith constitutes the groundwork of the Church which was later organized. If this first vision was but a figment of Joseph Smith's imagination, then the Mormon church is what its detractors declare it to be—a wicked and deliberate imposture [*The Abundant Life,* 310–311].

Further reading: CCC 65–67, IM, chapter 28 and appendix II.

12. Genealogy

(Use for Discussion 6)

"[T]he greatest responsibility in this world that God has laid upon us, is to seek after our dead," because we cannot be saved without them [Joseph Fielding Smith, DS 2:149].

Mormons are expected to redeem the dead. They believe that all who die outside the Mormon church will be given the opportunity to hear the "true gospel" while they are in "spirit prison." Should they accept it, they must be "baptized" into the Mormon church and receive all its other ordinances by proxy. Only then will they have the opportunity to enjoy eternal life.

This belief explains the church's avid interest in genealogical research. Each member is expected to know or trace his family tree back at least four generations and do further research if possible. He is to find the names of his immediate ancestors and as much other information as possible, including their dates of birth, marriage, and death. The member is then responsible for submitting these names to the temple so that the proxy work may be done for each family member.

"Avoid Foolish Questions, and Genealogies"

Paul, writing to Titus (3:9), instructs Christians to eschew the making of foolish genealogies. He had similarly written to Timothy, urging him not to "give heed to fables and endless genealogies" (1 Tim. 1:4). Despite Paul's explicit instruction, the Mormon church has proceeded to build the largest genealogical library in the world. Mormons expect one day to have a complete genealogy of the human race, comprising billions of names and listing every human ever to exist, all the way back to Adam.

Trying to justify its unbiblical practice, Mormonism appeals to a number of Scripture passages:

> Else what shall they do which are baptized for the dead, if the dead rise not at all? why are they then baptized for the dead? [I Cor. 15:29].

This is the verse Mormons use to support their practice of proxy baptism for the dead. As the *Encyclopedia of Mormonism* (vol. 2) admits, there is no other New Testament or early Christian evidence to support proxy baptism, which was never part of orthodox Christian practice. Nor can 1 Corinthians 15:29 support it. In the chapter, Paul is defending the general resurrection—the fact that we will all one day rise again, just as Jesus did. In the process of making his case, he tosses in the reference to baptism and the dead.

He does not tell us who is being baptized in relation to the dead. He only refers to these people as "they." It may be a group of heretics or even non-Christians. (Many Jews of the period practiced forms of baptism.) All he is doing is pointing out that the baptismal practice of some people presupposes the future resurrection. But even assuming he is talking about some kind of proxy baptism, one cannot claim that Paul is supporting the practice.

Another explanation sees this verse referring to the practice of catechumens stepping forward to be baptized for—that is, inspired by—the heroic witness of martyred Christians. Most likely, the passage is a reference to pagans who embrace the Christian faith and are baptized in order to be united with their dead Christian loved ones in the next life. They will be disappointed if there is no resurrection from the dead, no intermediate state before that, and this life is all there is.

In any case, one obscure reference hardly serves as a foundation to justify Mormonism's vast genealogical and temple systems.

> For Christ also hath once suffered for sins, the just for the unjust, that he might bring us to God, being put to death in the flesh, but quickened by the Spirit: By which also he went and preached unto the spirits in prison [I Pet. 3:18–19].

"For this cause was the gospel preached also to them that are dead" (1 Pet. 4:6).

Mormons teach that the "spirits in prison" to whom Christ preached while his body lay in the tomb were all the dead who would now hear the Christian (actually, Mormon) message and could request proxy baptism. But the texts do not support this conclusion.

There are several possible interpretations of these texts, but for the sake of argument, let us assume that the group of spirits in prison from 1 Peter 3:18 are the same as the group of "the dead" mentioned in 1 Peter 4:6,[1] that this group died because of their sins during the age of Noah, that they had the gospel preached to them by Christ during the three days he lay in the tomb, and that they are saved. None of this requires that they were given a "second chance" after death.

Scripture condemns the idea that there is a second chance after death. Hebrews 9:27 is clear: "It is appointed unto men once to die, but after this the judgment." Jesus also tells us there is an un-bridgeable gulf between those in heaven and those in hell (Luke 16:19–31). The place and time to work out our salvation is here and now (2 Cor. 6:2). Any interpretation of 1 Peter 3 and 4 that implies a chance to repent after death is wrong.

But there is no need for such an interpretation. On the assumptions made above, the dead in these passages would consist of those who disobeyed during the time of Noah, for whose sins the flood came on the world. However, the group under discussion was not worthy of damnation, either because they repented as the flood-waters rose or because they sinned grievously enough to warrant the severe temporal punishment of death but not grievously

---

[1] The spirits mentioned may be angelic rather than human spirits, depending on the interpretation of Gen. 6:1–2. Cf. W. J. Dalton, S.J., *Christ's Procla-mation to the Spirits* (Rome: 1965). Similarly, "the dead" may be a reference to Christians who were alive at the time they heard the gospel but who have now died. Nevertheless, for the sake of argument, we will assume that both of these groups are the same and that they are human spirits.

enough to warrant the even more severe, eternal punishment of damnation. Their behavior was not enough to grant them safety in the ark, but not enough to put them in hell.

Consequently, they waited in the place of the dead until the coming of Christ, who opened heaven to them, that they might "live according to God in the spirit" (1 Pet. 4:6). The preaching of the gospel in this case was what it was to ancient Israel—the announcement of the good news that the expected Messiah had come.

The gospel was not simply a message given to encourage people to seek eternal life. The righteous in Israel were already leading devout and holy lives and were already in God's grace. The righteous dead received the good news in the same way as the righteous in Israel: It was a time of joy signaling the blessings of the Messianic age, which for the dead meant getting to go to heaven. It was only fitting that this good news should be announced to them.

Further reading: CCC 946–962, 1030–1032; *IM,* chapters 7 and 24.

13. God

(Use for Discussion 1)

Of all Mormonism's errors, its aberrant teachings on the nature and person of God most fly in the face of orthodox Christianity and monotheism itself. Mormons are polytheists. They believe in more than one God. They also maintain God the Father was once a mortal man and possesses a body of flesh and bone.

God the Father Possesses a Physical Body

The Mormon church teaches that "the Father has a body of flesh and bones as tangible as man's" (D&C 130:22). Smith, at the end of his life, taught that

> God was once as we are now, and is an exalted man, and sits enthroned in yonder heavens! That is the great secret. If the veil were rent today, and the great God who holds this world in its orbit, and who upholds all worlds and all things by his power, was to make himself visible—I say, if you were to see him today, you would see him like a man in form—like yourselves in all the person, image, and very form as a man [*TPJS*, 344–345].

Ask the missionaries about Smith's teachings. Otherwise, they may not tell you. When you press them for some kind of biblical support for such a notion, expect them to cite several passages:

> And God said, Let us make man in our image. . . . So God created man in his own image, in the image of God created he him, male and female created he them [Gen. 1:26–27].

79

Mormons suppose that the image of God is physical. However, the image of God in man, like the image of God in the angels, is not a physical likeness but a spiritual one. God is a rational Spirit (John 4:24), not having a physical form (Luke 24:39), and so any being with a rational soul is like him and "in his image" compared to non-rational, purely material creation.

And the Lord spake unto Moses face to face, as a man speaketh unto his friend [Ex. 33:11].

If there be a prophet among you, I the Lord will make myself known unto him in a vision, and will speak unto him in a dream. My servant Moses is not so, who is faithful in all mine house. With him I will speak mouth to mouth, even apparently, and not in dark speeches; and the similitude of the Lord shall he behold [Num. 12:6–8].

The Mormon idea that God spoke to Moses directly, in a physical body, is contradicted later in the same chapter containing the first of these two verses. In Exodus 33:20, God tells Moses that he will allow his glory to pass before him, but that no one can see him and live. Thus Moses *had not seen God*. If he had seen anything at all, it would have been a theophany, in which God temporarily assumed a visible form to facilitate communication with a human.

More likely, as the parallel passage in Numbers 12 suggests, the metaphors "face to face" and "mouth to mouth" mean that God communicated with Moses in a plain and direct fashion, not in the "dark speeches" ("riddles," NAB) he uses to speak to most prophets. The use of such metaphors is in keeping with Hebrew speech. All the passages show is the contrasting modes God uses in communicating with his prophets. Most will receive his word through dreams and visions, but the Lord will deal with Moses when he is alert, not asleep or in a trance.

Mormons also commonly point to verses that use anthropomorphic language when speaking of God, speaking metaphorically of the arm of the Lord, the eyes of the Lord, the mouth of the Lord, etc. This language is no surprise in Scripture. The ancient Hebrews had a concrete idiom, rich in metaphor, and they frequently used anthropomorphic language to describe God as well as other things (Ps. 85:10, where the concepts of mercy, truth, righteousness and peace are anthropomorphized).

In the case of God, he knew all things, so his "eyes" searched all mankind. He was everywhere present and could do all things, so the powerful "hand" of the Lord embraced all his creation. He delivered Israel in battle, so the victory was said to be won by the Lord's mighty "arm." These passages cannot be used to build up a composite, physical picture of God any more than other biblical passages that speak of God as having feathers and wings (Ps. 91:4; also, Ps. 17:8, 36:7, 57:1, 61:4, 63:7), as a fire and a furnace (Deut. 4:24; Zech. 2:5; Heb. 12:29), or as a rock (Deut. 32:4; 2 Sam. 22:2).

On the other hand, you can show the missionaries the true nature of God from scriptural texts they ignore.

God is not a man that he should lie; neither the son of man, that he should repent [Num. 23:19].

I am God, and not man [Hos. 11:9].

While Mormons believe God is an exalted man, these two passages make it clear that he's not a man at all.

God is a Spirit: and they that worship him must worship him in spirit and in truth [John 4:24].

A spirit hath not flesh and bones [Luke 24:39].

Christ defines God and spirit. God is a spirit, and a spirit is immaterial. Therefore, God is not composed of matter and possesses no sort of body. Humans, who possess a body and a spirit, must worship God in spirit. That is, the infinite God, because he is not limited by a material body, is present everywhere and may be "reached" by anyone at any time and in any place.

Thou canst not see my face: for there shall be no man see me, and live [Ex. 33:20].

No man hath seen God at any time; the only begotten Son, which is in the bosom of the Father, he hath declared him [John 1:18].

Mormons deal with such verses by ignoring them or, in Smith's case, altering them to permit a select few—principally himself—to see the Lord and live. But this is not what the text says.

God Became God

Get the missionaries to tell you where God's physical body came from. It's not part of their first discussion, even though Mormons assert a correct knowledge of God's character is vital for salvation.

What Mormons must tell you, if pressed, is that God was once a mortal man in some other world. He was born of mortal parents and lived a faithful "Mormon" life there. After his death, he was resurrected by his own god and worked his way to his own divinity. Upon achieving godhood, his god gave him the right to create this and many other worlds. He, with his heavenly wives (also resurrected women), procreated spirit children and eventually put them into the human bodies created here by our human parents.

There Are Gods without Number

How many Gods there are, I do not know. But there never was a time when there were not Gods and worlds. . . . That course has been from all eternity, and it is and will be to all eternity [*Discourses of Brigham Young*, 22].

The second Mormon prophet here merely echoes the later teachings of his predecessor, Smith, who said the Bible itself taught a "plurality of Gods beyond the power of refutation" (*TPJS*, 372). Smith and his followers believe they find biblical justification for their polytheism in the following passages.

And God said, Let us make man in our image. . . . So God
created man in his own image, in the image of God created
he him; male and female created he them [Gen. 1:26-27].

Because the Hebrew word for God here is *Elohim*, a plural noun,
Mormons conclude that there is a plurality of divine beings. This
ignores the fact that the Hebrew term *Elohim* is regularly used as
a name for the one true God in Scripture. Even Mormons admit
this (asserting that *Elohim* is the particular name of God the Father). But once this is admitted, one cannot read Genesis 1:26-
27 as if it is a reference to multiple gods.

Verse 26 may refer to "us" and "our," but this in no way requires multiple gods. It may be the royal plural used by monarchs
to refer to themselves, it may be God the Father addressing the
other two persons of the Trinity or it may be God announcing
his intention before the angels of heaven. However that may be,
the rest of verses 26 and 27 are in the singular: "God created
man in his [singular] own image. . . ." The verb "created" and
the following "he" and "his" are all singular. This shows us that
the term *Elohim* here, as so often elsewhere in Scripture, is being
used as a name for the one true God, not as a reference to multiple
gods.

God standeth in the congregation of the mighty; he judgeth
among the gods [Ps. 82:1ff].

Jesus answered them, Is it not written in your law, I said, Ye
are gods? [John 10:34].

The Mormon misuse of these passages, like the previous one,
is based on a failure to recognize how a word is used in Scripture.
The Hebrew term *Elohim*, apart from being a personal name for
the true God and apart from being a reference to pagan gods,
is also sometimes a reference to human judges. The situation is
analogous to the English term "Lord," which sometimes refers
to God and sometimes refers to magistrates, including judges in
the British court system. Nobody supposes, when a barrister in a

British court refers to the judge as "My lord," that he is attributing divinity to him.

In Psalm 82, a play on words is used between *Elohim* as a proper name for God and *elohim* as a reference to human judges. The play on words is used to highlight an ironic contrast between God as the ultimate Just Judge and the unjust human judges whom he condemns in the psalm. These would themselves die and be judged (82:7).

Jesus' use of Psalm 82 (John 10:34) does not go beyond the psalm's meaning and simply shows that the term "elohim" can in particular circumstances be used to refer to men without blasphemy. His argument has an *a fortiori* ("how much more") form. In essence, it is: If even unjust mere human judges can be called *elohim*, how much more can *I* be called *elohim*. And, of course, Jesus can be called *Elohim* in the ultimate sense, because he really *is* God.

> For though there be [those] that are called gods, whether in heaven or in earth, (as there be gods many, and lords many) [1 Cor. 8:5].

"Look here," the Mormon will say. "Even Paul admits there are many gods."

No, he doesn't. Though he does say there are those that are called gods. You must read the entire context. The whole chapter teaches mature Christians not to give scandal to the weaker members. Most of the Corinthian Christians were recent converts from a paganism that included animal sacrifice in its rituals. The meat offered to idols was then sold in the marketplace. Paul was asked if a Christian could buy and eat such meat. He responds in verse 4 by maintaining that "there is none other God but one," and again in verse 6 by saying "there is but one God." Therefore, meat offered to other "gods" is really nothing special, and a Christian could eat it. But don't buy it, though, if by doing so you would give scandal to the immature Christians.

The "gods many, and lords many" exist only as idols and other pagan divinities. For example, the sun, moon, and stars were worshipped by pagans as gods. Verse 5, used by the Mormons to justify their belief in many gods, is sandwiched between two verses that plainly teach absolute monotheism.

What the missionaries may tell you is that, though there are innumerable gods, we are to worship only one, called the Heavenly Father. But to say there are uncounted other deities is to deny to the true God his oneness, uniqueness, and infinity. Moreover, to say that the God we worship has a father and god whom he worships (and a grandfather and god, and so forth), is to deny the Lord's supremacy.

> He [St. Stephen, the first martyr], being full of the Holy Ghost, looked up steadfastly into heaven, and saw the glory of God, and Jesus standing on the right hand of God [Acts 7:55–56].

A Mormon missionary will say: "There it is—visual proof of both God the Father's corporeality and a plurality of gods." But Stephen doesn't see God's body, but his glory, his majesty. Thus John could later say, "No man hath seen God at any time" (1 John 4:11a). That *includes* Stephen's vision, in which Jesus' authority is displayed by metaphorically showing him at God's "right hand" —the place of honor, power and privilege. The passage thus does not assert that God the Father has a physical body (it was a *vision* to begin with), and while it shows that there are two divine persons, it does not show that there are two gods. The Father and the Son are two distinct persons of the Trinity, the one true God. Merely pointing to two persons of the Trinity does not prove the existence of more than one God.

The problem with Mormon misuse of these and similar passages is their almost universal misunderstanding of the Christian doctrine of the Trinity. They seem to think we're modalists— believing in one God who is only one person. Therefore, they scoff at the idea that God could be praying to himself in the garden, or descending upon himself at the Jordan. But, in fact, Catholics *don't* believe that the Son prayed to himself (he prayed to a different divine person—the Father) or that the Son descended on himself (a different divine person—the Spirit—did so). Most Mormons take no time to study a doctrine they dismiss as absurd.

Christian Response

Brigham Young challenged, "Take up the Bible, compare the religion of the Latter-day Saints with it, and see if it will stand the test" (*JD* 16:46).

We'll do just that. The following passages are representative of the Christian teaching that there is one God, a Trinity of persons and unity of nature, who is unlimited and unequaled. You may wish to mark these verses and have them ready when a Mormon calls.

1. *There is only one God:* Deut. 4:35, 6:4, 32:39; 2 Sam. 7:22; 1 Kgs. 8:60; Ps. 86:10; Is. 43:10–11, 44:6, 8; Hos. 13:4; John 17:3; 1 Cor. 8:4; Gal. 3:20; Eph. 4:6; 1 Tim. 1:17, 2:5; James 2:9; Jude 25.

2. *God is unbounded:* 1 Kgs. 8:27; Ps. 148:13; Jer. 23:24; Acts 7:48–49.

3. *God is all-present:* Ps. 139:7; Is. 57:15; Jer. 23:24; Amos 9:2–3; Eph. 1:23.

4. *God is all-powerful:* Gen. 17:1, 28:3, 35:11, 43:14; Ex. 6:3; Rev. 1:8, 4:8, 11:17, 16:14, 21:22.

5. *God is eternal:* Gen. 21:33; Deut. 32:40; Ps. 33:11, 90:1; Is. 26:4, 44:6; Hab. 1:2; Rom. 16:26; 1 Tim. 1:17; Rev. 4:8.

6. *God is all-knowing:* 1 Kgs. 8:39; Job 9:4, 37:16; Ps. 33:13, 139:1ff; Is. 44:7ff; Mt. 6:8; Acts 1:24; Rom. 11:33; Heb. 4:13; 1 John 3:19.

7. *God is unchanging:* Num. 23:19; 1 Sam. 15:29; Ps. 33:11, 102:26; Is. 14:24; Mt. 24:35; Heb. 6:17; Jas. 1:17.

The finite, changeable Mormon God is not the God of the Bible, of the Church Fathers and Tradition or even of the Book of Mormon. He is a product of Smith's later thoughts, as changeable as most other Mormon doctrines.

Particularly useful for refuting the Mormon view of God are the passages given below from the book of Isaiah. In these, God not only declares that he is the only God, he says that he, an omniscient or all-knowing Being, knows of the existence of no other God, that no God was formed before him and that no God will be formed after him.

To whom then will ye liken me, or shall I be equal? saith the Holy One [Is. 40:25].

I am the LORD: that is my name: and my glory will I not give to another [Is. 42:8].

I am he: before me there was no God formed, neither shall there be after me [Is. 43:10].

I am the first, and I am the last; and beside me there is no God. . . . Is there a God beside me? yea, there is no God; I know not any [Is. 44:6, 8].

I am the LORD, and there is none else, there is no God beside me [Is. 45:5].

I am God, and there is none else; I am God, and there is none like me [Is. 46:9].

Further reading: CCC 198–324, 370, 2807–2815; *TB*, chapters 2–6; *IM*, chapters 17, 18, and 21.

14. The Holy Ghost

(*Use for Discussions 1 and 2*)

According to Joseph Fielding Smith, "The Holy Ghost is the third member of the Godhead. He is a Spirit, in the form of a man. . . . As a spirit personage the Holy Ghost has size and dimensions. He does not fill the immensity of space, and cannot be everywhere present in person at the same time" [*DS* 1:38].

The Holy Ghost is, in fact, a third Mormon god, subordinate to the Father and the Son. (See President Heber C. Kimball, *JD* 5:180.) He was created, as was the Son, at some point in the distant past. Unlike the other two gods, the Holy Ghost does not have a physical body, though some Mormon scholars maintain he will have to be incarnated at some future point. Rather, he now possesses a "spirit body" in the shape and dimensions of a man's. Like the other gods, the Holy Ghost is limited and changeable. He cannot be all-present, since his "spirit body" allows him to be in only one place at one time.

Early Mormon Teachings Ignored the Holy Ghost

Smith originally taught there were two "personages who constitute the great, matchless, governing, and supreme power over all things. . . . They are the Father and the Son. . . ." The Holy Ghost was described merely as the "mind" of the two. (See *Lectures on Faith*, lecture five.) A few years later, Smith changed his doctrine to view the Holy Ghost as a personal being. (See D&C 130:22.)

Appealing to the Holy Ghost
Trumps Science, Reason, and Facts

Maybe you've already encountered the frustration so common in speaking with Mormons. When you demonstrate from Scripture, historical, and scientific fact and common sense that certain of their beliefs are contradictory or impossible, they often counter by "bearing their testimony." No matter how many versions Smith's alleged First Vision went through, Mormon members "know" it happened in just the way the "official" rendition has it, because they have been told so by the Holy Ghost. Never mind that Scripture conclusively teaches there are no other gods. The Mormon "feels" in his heart that Mormon writings constitute a valid corrective to the Bible's errors. And while abortion is, as their leaders have said, the crime of killing unborn children, Mormons accept it because they have a "testimony" of the divine approval of these same leaders, who have recently discovered several loopholes.

There's no accounting for "testimonies." Earnest and honest missionaries will bear their testimony about any aspect of church doctrine or practice. They "know" that Smith was a prophet, therefore, all he taught is pure and true. They "bear witness" that the present head of the church is also a divinely appointed prophet, so everything he teaches is also true—no matter that it may contradict Smith or other earlier leaders.

In all this, the Holy Ghost gets the credit for ongoing revelation. As times and circumstances change, so do his divine laws.

God Is the Same Yesterday, Today, and Forever

"God is not the author of confusion, but of peace," Paul told the Corinthians (1 Cor. 14:33). The Holy Ghost could not have told the early leaders of the Mormon church one thing and then contradicted himself later with more recent prophets. The Spirit of God cannot inspire Brigham Young to teach Adam is God and Spencer W. Kimball to call that a false doctrine. The Spirit of God cannot teach that blacks will not hold the priesthood until the Second Coming and now admit them. Nor can he teach that polygamy is required for eternal salvation and then, forty-five years later, make it grounds for excommunication. He does not inspire church leaders to relax their position on abortion, contraception and divorce in order to keep pace with the times.

If a Mormon missionary or member attempts to end a discussion by bearing his testimony about this thing or that, recognize it for what it is: a subjective declaration of emotion being chalked up to God. All one needs to establish the unreliability of such Mormon "testimonies" is to look at the disastrous record of doctrinal reversals their church has made. The subjective testimonies being given by members today are no more valid than those given by their forebears in support of a different set of doctrines.

You might counter their bearing of subjective testimony by bearing your own testimony and then backing it up with objective evidence. A good way to start would be to tell the missionaries, "I testify to you that there is but one God, who is a Trinity of equal and eternal persons. He is unchanging and unbounded. His Son, Jesus Christ, founded the Catholic Church to last till the end of time, establishing the papacy with St. Peter. I know that all the Church teaches is true, because Christ said of it, 'He who hears you hears me.' I say all this in the name of Jesus Christ. Amen."

Further reading: CCC 687–747; *IM*, chapter 20.

15. Jesus Christ

(Use for Discussions 1, 2, and 6)

Mormon missionaries will tell you the following about Jesus: He is God, he is the only-begotten Son of the Heavenly Father, by his suffering and death, we have forgiveness of our sins and faith in him is necessary for salvation. By insisting on these four points, Mormons expect to convince you they are worthy of the name "Christian."

But here's what they usually don't tell you:

1. Jesus Christ is a subordinate, lesser god than the Father (and the Holy Ghost is lower still).

By obedience and devotion to the truth, he [Jesus Christ] attained that pinnacle of intelligence which ranked him as a God, as the Lord Omnipotent, while yet in his pre-existent state [*MD*, 129].

Note that this passage discusses Christ's gradual "progress" to godhood during the ages before he took flesh. In other words, there was a time when he was not God. He, who called himself "the way, the truth, and the life," had to learn the way to the truth and eternal life. Note, too, that the Son is called *a* god, one among many.

Also, though the Mormon church calls Jesus God, Mormons are not permitted to pray to him. All prayer is to go directly to the Father, in the name of the Son. Nor may Christ the Lord be worshipped as Almighty God. But this contradicts such biblical evidence as presented in Matthew's Gospel, where we see the magi, the leper, the Canaanite woman, the women disciples and all the disciples "worshipping" Christ. (See Matt. 2:11, 8:2, 9:18, 15:25, 28:9, 17. See also John 9:38, 20:28; Rev. 4:10, 5:14.)

2. Jesus Christ is, according to Mormons, the only-begotten Son of the Father.

This sounds right until you press a bit further. Mormonism teaches God the Father and his heavenly wife or wives procreated the billions of spirits that would eventually be placed in the bodies created by earthly parents. So, at some point in the distant past, each of us came into personal, conscious existence and lived in heavenly mansions under the tutelage of our divine parents before coming to earth. Jesus was the very first of these spirit children, though not unique. He is, in that way, our "elder brother." Now, don't be misled. We also believe that Christ existed before his Incarnation. But he was not procreated by a Heavenly Father and mother. Rather, he existed as God from all eternity. No divine copulation was needed to produce him.

Further, the term "only-begotten" doesn't refer to this spirit existence. It can't, since Mormons think we all came into being in the same way. What Mormons do think it refers to is their idea that Christ was the only-begotten of the Father *in the flesh*—i.e., that God the Father begot Jesus in the flesh through copulation with the Virgin Mary. The Mormon teaching is that

> God the Father is a perfected, glorified, holy Man, an immortal Personage. And Christ was born into the world as the literal Son of this Holy Being; he was born in the same personal, real, and literal sense that any mortal son is born to a mortal father. There is nothing figurative about his paternity; he was begotten, conceived and born in the normal and natural course of events, for he is the Son of God, and that designation means what it says [*MD*, 742].

Since their earliest years Mormons have taught that

> the fleshly body of Jesus required a Mother as a well as a Father. Therefore, the Father and Mother of Jesus, according

to the flesh, must have been associated together in the capacity of Husband and Wife: hence the Virgin Mary must have been, for the time being, the lawful wife of God the Father [Orson Pratt, *The Seer*, 158–159].

Though Mormons say they believe Christ was born of the "Virgin" Mary, they must resort to redefinition. Mormon apostle McConkie twists the term to mean someone who has not had sexual intercourse with a *mortal* man. Since God the Father was by then immortal, he and Mary could engage in literal sexual intercourse without loss to her "virginity." (See *The Mortal Messiah*, vol. 1, 314.) Of course, this is ridiculous. Sex is sex, whether it is with an immortal man or a mortal man.

Needless to say, you won't find a shred of biblical (or patristic) support for this blasphemous absurdity.

3. In the Mormon view, there are important limitations on Christ's atonement.

First, Christ's redemption, in itself, merely grants the resurrection of the body and its reunion with the spirit. This, to Mormonism, is the "general salvation" granted freely to all men. It is a strange idea, given the Mormon concept of the eternity of spirit and matter. But let that pass for now.

Second, and more important, is the Mormon belief that the Lord's shed blood and death is not sufficient to forgive every sin. There are some sins for which even his redemption is inadequate. These include murder and apostasy from the Mormon church. If one guilty of such crimes is to have any chance for redemption, his own blood must be shed in atonement. This contradicts the Bible's assertion that

the blood of Jesus Christ his Son cleanseth us from all sin [1 John 1:7b].

Married . . . with Children

Though it's not official doctrine (yet), many Mormons believe Jesus was married, and to several women at that. He also fathered children with his plural wives.

> It will be borne in mind that once on a time, there was a marriage in Cana in Galilee; and on a careful reading of that transaction, it will be discovered that no less a person than Jesus Christ was married on that occasion. If he was never married, his intimacy with Mary and Martha, and the other Mary also whom Jesus loved, must have been highly unbecoming and improper to say the best of it [Apostle Orson Hyde, *JD* 4:259].

This early apostle's beliefs have been echoed throughout the years among leadership and members alike. Christ had to have a wife and children if he were to fulfill all the divine commands. It was his polygamy that led to his death, according to early Mormon president Jedediah M. Grant.

> "The grand reason of the burst of public sentiment in anathemas upon Christ and his disciples, causing his crucifixion," Grant said, "was evidently based upon polygamy, according to the testimony of the philosophers who rose in that age. A belief in the doctrine of a plurality of wives caused the persecution of Jesus and his followers" [*JD* 1:346].

The Bible and historic Christian teaching give no support whatsoever to such ideas. Scripture and Tradition make it clear that the Bride of Christ is the Church (Eph. 5:23; Rev. 21:9–10), not an individual human woman, much less a harem.

"Another Testament . . ."

One way in which the Mormon church has tried to make its image more Christian is by adding a subtitle to its Book of Mormon, now calling it "Another Testament of Jesus Christ." It's true that Christ is mentioned frequently in the book, though the specifically Mormon views presented above are not found within its pages. Although the book is not particularly offensive in its treatment of Christ, at least when compared to what Mormons *really* teach concerning Christ, the church that distributes it shouldn't expect a subtitle to cover up its many demeaning, heretical doctrines about the Savior. A more apt description could be "Testament to Another Christ."

Apostle Bruce R. McConkie to BYU Students:

Though Christ is God, yet there is a Deity above him, a Deity whom he worships. . . . All of us, Christ included, seek to become like the Father. In this sense the First-born, our Elder Brother, goes forward as we do ["Our Relationship with the Lord," 6–7].

Further reading: CCC 422–682; *IM*, chapter 19; *TB*, chapters 11 and 12.

16. Joseph Smith

(*Use for Discussion 1*)

> Mormonism, as it is called, must stand or fall on the story of Joseph Smith. He was either a prophet of God, divinely called, properly appointed and commissioned, or he was one of the biggest frauds this world has ever seen. There is no middle ground [Joseph Fielding Smith, *DS* 1:188].

The tenth Mormon prophet makes the challenge: Joseph Smith is a divinely ordained prophet or he is a malicious fake. We might quibble that there are other options, such as Smith being a pitiable figure who was carried away by his own imagination and confusion, but the two basic options remain the same: Either Smith's claims were true or they were false. The evidence decisively shows the latter.

Brief Biography

The founder of Mormonism was born to Joseph Smith, Sr., and Lucy Mack Smith on December 23, 1805, in Sharon, Vermont. When Smith was about ten, his parents took him and his brothers and sisters to the area around Palmyra, in the Finger Lakes region of New York. Smith grew up in a Protestant area. He did not receive Catholic theological formation, and it is no surprise that contemporary Mormonism still bears an unmistakably Protestant stamp, though it has greatly departed from historic Protestant belief. Smith later claimed, though the evidence does not bear out the assertion, that there was great revival and controversy among the different Protestant churches of the region. The ensuing religious confusion supposedly drove Smith to pray concerning which church he should join. Smith claimed, in response to this, that he received at age fourteen a revelation that all Christian churches were corrupt and that he would be called upon to bring back the Lord's lost church. A few years later, he said he was led to discover golden plates written in a strange language. He was given supernatural power to translate the writings and produced the Book of Mormon in 1830, the same year he organized a church that would come to be known as the Mormon church.

Because of their strange beliefs and practices (multiple gods, multiple wives) and because they claimed divine right to lands already settled by others, the Mormons were driven out of western New York, Ohio, and Missouri, and settled for a time in Nauvoo, Illinois, on the banks of the Mississippi. There, Smith became a Mason and composed the Mormon temple ceremonies.

In addition to the Book of Mormon, Smith compiled the Doctrine and Covenants, a book containing alleged revelations from Christ. He also "translated" what he called the Book of Abraham from an ancient Egyptian papyrus and rewrote the Bible.

Several individuals published a newspaper critical of Smith. On Smith's orders, the dissidents' printing press was destroyed. He was arrested and jailed in Carthage, Illinois. His brother Hyrum and other church leaders were with him.

Hearing that the leader of the Mormon faction was in custody, a lynch mob stormed the jail. Hyrum Smith was shot and killed instantly. Joseph Smith, having obtained a smuggled six-shooter, blasted the attackers; some say he killed or wounded two of them. He was killed in the shoot-out. It was June 27, 1844; Smith was 38 years old. The Mormon church hails him as a martyr, even though he died trying to shoot others down in a gun battle.

Smith's Teachings and Prophecies

We needn't try to judge Smith as a man, but we must evaluate his religious claims: "Prove all things; hold fast that which is good" (1 Thess. 5:21). When we look at Smith's teachings, we find in them flagrant contradictions to God's written and oral word. Smith's later doctrines conflict with his earlier ones and his own successors in the office of prophet have frequently sought to distance themselves from some of his dictates. "That's only his opinion" is a common retort of the Mormon scholar when presented with Smith's (or Young's) indefensible positions. (But doesn't that seem odd? If I truly believed my church's leader was a prophet on the same level as Moses or Isaiah or Paul, wouldn't I hang on his every word? If he gave counsel, wouldn't I feel the safe course would be to follow it?)

Some of Smith's False Prophecies

1. D&C 84:1–5: In September 1832, Christ supposedly told Smith that "this generation shall not all pass away" until the "New Jerusalem" and temple be built by Mormons in Jackson County, Missouri. As of this date, there is no New Jerusalem or temple. (D&C 124:49–51 has the Lord changing his mind and excusing the Mormons from building it.)

2. D&C 84:114–119: Christ tells Smith that if the cities of New York, Albany, and Boston reject the Mormon gospel, "the hour of their judgment is nigh, and their house shall be left unto them desolate." After nearly 170 years, Mormonism is still a tiny sect in the American Northeast. And the three cities are still standing.

3. D&C 87:1–8 (given on December 25, 1832): This is a favorite of the missionaries. They say that here Smith prophesies the American Civil War nearly 30 years before its start. But South Carolina, mentioned in the "revelation," had six months earlier rejected Congressional tariffs in what is now known as the Nullification Crisis. By December 1832, the federal army was on alert. It didn't take a prophet to read the signs of the times. Indeed, even before Smith, Thomas Jefferson had predicted in 1820— as a matter of purely political estimation—that the Mis-

souri Compromise would prove "the knell of the Union" and lead eventually to a secession of the Southern states.

Smith's prophecy of the War between the States was nothing that wasn't being predicted by hundreds of others based on human judgment alone. When Smith went beyond this and tried to give his prediction the mantle of divine revelation, he got it wrong. The war did not break out for almost thirty years. When it did, there was no slave uprising (87:4) nor did it escalate into a world war so that "war will be poured out upon all nations, beginning at this place [South Carolina]" (87:2) nor did this world war continue until it "made a full end of all nations" (87:6). In hindsight, Smith's Civil War prophecy is laughably inaccurate.

4. D&C 114:1: On April 17, 1838, the Lord told Smith to have member David W. Patten settle his business affairs, since he would be called to go on a mission "next spring" (1839). Patten was killed in battle on October 25, 1838.

5. TPJS, 1843–1844, 286: "Were I going to prophesy, I would say the end [of the world] would not come in 1844, 5, or 6, or in forty years. There are those of the rising generation who shall not taste death till Christ comes." Those alive in 1844 are all dead by now. Christ has not returned.

There are many more prophecies and statements of Smith, Young and others that don't bear up. Some are embarrassing: that the sun and moon are inhabited. (See JD 13:270–271.) Or that Indian converts to Mormonism will find their skin turning from dark to "white and delightsome" (2 Nephi 30:6). With respect to this last prophecy, in the current edition of the Book of Mormon, the Mormon church has altered the revelation to read "pure and delightsome." When prophecies don't match reality, the Mormon strategy is to ignore them, explain them away, or even change them.

Further reading: IM, chapters 1 and 28.

17. Meetings

(*Use for Discussion 3*)

Inevitably, your Mormon missionaries or acquaintances will ask you to attend Sunday meetings with them. If you have nothing else to do for three or four hours on Sunday, if your Catholic faith is strong, and if the Mormons promise to spend the equivalent time with you at Sunday Mass and further discussion, you might consider going. Remember, if you're used to attending church as a family, you'll be separated for most of the Mormon meeting hours.

Also, be prepared for "love bombing." The members will welcome you warmly and urge you to return again and again. They'll sweet-talk you into attending other meetings later in the day or the week. And they'll coax you to be baptized. They can do this with a certain confidence, since most of their public gatherings are bland, supportive sessions devoid of the deeper, more surprising Mormon teachings.

The Sunday "block schedule" is composed of three consecutive meetings. It's significant that the Mormon church calls its Sunday gatherings "meetings" and not "worship." There's very little praise and worship in any Mormon gathering, either on Sundays or in the temples.

1. Sacrament Meeting

The most important of the three Sunday sessions is called the "sacrament meeting." It's either the first or last of the meetings and takes about seventy minutes; all attend as families. Except for an opening and closing "spontaneous" prayer from a member, a few hymns and the passing around of bread and water, most of the time is devoted to talks delivered by members of the congregation.

The talks may be on such diverse topics as Joseph Smith, a Book of Mormon character, growing a garden, keeping a journal, or the resurrection. Speakers depend on what they perceive as the promptings of the Holy Ghost to give them the words to say.

The only brief break from all the talking is the ritual pronunciation of a blessing over commercial bread slices and small cups of water. Mormons reject Christ's Eucharistic teaching in the Last Supper accounts and John 6. They consider their "sacrament" to be merely a memorial of Christ's work on their behalf and a reminder of the promises they made to live up to Mormon rules.

2. Sunday School

For about 45 minutes, the membership attends age-appropriate "Gospel Doctrine" classes.

3. Priesthood, Relief Society, Young Women's Meetings

The third hour is also segregated by age and by sex.

Testimonies, Left and Right

Every member is expected, at some point, to bear his testimony of the "restored church." Sunday meetings are the most likely occasion, and you'll notice that most speakers conclude their remarks with "I testify to this . . . in the name of Jesus Christ. Amen."

Instead of worship, Mormon meetings emphasize mutual encouragement and promotion. By hearing a steady flow of "I know this church (Book of Mormon, Joseph Smith, tithing, etc.) is true," the members feel supported in their own beliefs. While corporate sacrifice and worship defines the Catholic Mass, corporate coaching and motivation marks most Mormon gatherings.

Restoration of Early Church Worship?

Because it claims its doctrines and practices replicate those of the earliest church members—those in apostolic times—we'd expect to see the same pattern of Sunday meetings in the Acts of the Apostles as we see in Mormon wards. But we don't. Not even close.

The early Christians gathered to hear and study the Word of God (Acts 17:11; also John 5:39).

Mormons rarely read publicly from the Bible or even their own scriptures. Nor do they usually address scripture topics in sermons.

The early Christians corporately worshipped Christ and his Father (Acts 2:42–47).

While Mormonism permits the worship of God the Father, it is almost never done in a public, communal setting. Except for a brief opening and closing prayer and a few hymns, little else is addressed to the Lord.

The early Christians shared in the Eucharist, believing it to be a sharing in Christ's body and blood (1 Cor. 11:23–29).

Mormons eat a piece of bread and sip some water as mere reminders of their promises to live good Mormon lives.

Quid Pro Quo

Remember, if you do decide to attend the Sunday meetings, first take the missionaries to Mass. Discuss the Eucharistic liturgy with them. Show them the biblical and patristic basis for our worship. (See *CCC* 1345–1347 for a good discussion of Mass in the early Church.) Remind them that, unless they "eat the flesh of the Son of man, and drink his blood," neither they nor their worship have life in them (John 6:53).

Further reading: CCC 1322–1419; *IM*, chapters 4 and 5; *CF*, chapters 19 and 20; *TB*, chapters 17 and 18.

18. Missionary Work

(*Use for Discussion 6*)

Mormons are obligated to preach their religion and recruit as many converts as they can, in order to save themselves and their new members. Those who hear the Mormon "gospel" and reject it ("the wicked") have no further hope of salvation.

Not for Missionaries Only

If you've ever felt "pestered" by a Mormon acquaintance, realize that he is simply working out his ultimate godhood by trying to lengthen the membership rolls of his church.

The Official Missionaries

In addition to the Mormon apostles and members of the "Seventies," who are paid by the Mormon church, thousands of others devote a year or two of their lives in full-time missionary work. The majority of these are young men, at least nineteen years of age, who volunteer to serve for two years in any of the mission districts established throughout the world. A smaller number of young women, in their early twenties, also serve for eighteen months. In recent years, older married couples and singles have also been called to fill leadership positions. Many also work in various Mormon offices, temples, and visitors' centers throughout the world.

In theory, the missionary is asked to pay for his or her own time in the mission field. Young men, for instance, are asked to pay about $400 a month. Those unable to pay are subsidized by their local congregations and by the church.

Newer recruits are paired with the more senior missionaries.

Most young "elders" and "sisters" are transferred to other districts within their mission territory every few months. Most missions have a hundred or more missionaries who are directed by a missionary president and his wife. This couple is given the use of a house and car.

Periodic meetings are held to check on individual and group progress. The more productive missionaries are given higher status and greater authority. To be a "returned missionary," one who has honorably discharged his duties, generally opens doors back home, after the missionary has returned to regular life.

"Building Relationships of Trust"

Notice when you invite a missionary team into your home. They'll probably look around for family photographs, books, toys, trophies or other objects they can use to introduce their Mormon pitch about "families first" and "families can be forever." They've been taught to "build relationships of trust" with a potential convert. They're told something like: "Get to know your target, get him to like and trust you. Talk about your own family and feelings. Then gradually introduce the pre-selected and pre-packaged message you were taught in the missionary training program." (See the Mormon *Missionary Guide: Training for Missionaries*, 60ff.)

Unsuspecting non-Mormons, swayed by the missionaries' apparent affection and concern, are anticipated to later say things like, "They put a lot of effort into making me feel comfortable. . . . I was touched they would share their deepest feelings with me. I respect and admire them for that" (ibid., 61).

Giving "warm fuzzies" to potential converts might not be the way to introduce them to the "only true church in the whole world," yet this is what the missionaries do best. Any extended questioning of them would reveal an almost universal ignorance of Mormon theology, history, or practice. While they have been taught proof texts from the Bible and their own scriptures, they are in the dark concerning contradicting passages and analysis.

Presenting the Six Discussions

The natural flow of the pre-packaged instructions the missionaries are trained to deliver is meant to be light, inspiring, and inoffensive. By building on what they think is common ground (belief in one God, the divinity of Christ, and an after-life), the Mormon representatives try to get you to accept the logical conclusion that theirs is the Lord's only church, fulfilling all the requirements they say it should. This is all circular reasoning, as can be seen in a brief experiment:

Don't be satisfied with letting the missionaries control the direction of the discussions. If you've decided to give them a hearing, they'll start with the first discussion, which contains a half-dozen major topics ripe for your Catholic critique. The first part of this book discussed how you can bring the Mormon missionary machine to a screeching halt by *concentrating* on any one of those subjects. Rather than let the missionaries lecture on blandly about "one eternal and infinite God," for instance, stop them and present them with information you've discovered in this book that they haven't told you. Make them respond satisfactorily (they won't be able to) and don't let them change the subject.

Then, since they're already there, bear *your* "testimony" to the true faith and explain God from the Scriptures and Catholic teachings. Do this with every topic they bring up.

However, while their message should be rejected, they are God's children and loved by him. We must act toward them in a caring and Christ-like manner. Part of that involves showing them their errors and giving them the opportunity to come to the truth. Slamming a door on them does not do that. On the other hand, don't open that door unless you're prepared to deal with them from a position of strong faith. God does not call people to evangelize when they are not first strong in their own faith.

Further reading: CCC 849–856, 905.

19. Plan of Salvation

(*Use for Discussions 1 and 4*)

When Mormons speak of "the gospel," they don't mean the "good news" of Jesus Christ as explained in the Gospels. Nor do they refer to the proclamation that Divine Providence has given us a way to find forgiveness for our sins and a way to eternal life. What they mean is the "plan of salvation" as developed by the Mormon church.

The missionaries and other Mormons will likely be reluctant to explain the plan of salvation, especially in one hearing, but to be a good Mormon, you must believe each of the following points:

1. There is no such thing as immaterial spirit. Everything is matter, even what we call "spirit," which is just a more highly refined matter.

2. All matter is eternal, unmade, and indestructible. All components that make up man, animals, plants, earth, sea and sky, the planets, and God himself have existed from forever.

3. At some point in time, some (other) god "organized" a world out of pre-existing elements. At the same time and in the same way, he created a man and a woman who would populate that world. (This is not to be confused with Adam and Eve, who would come much later.)

4. Unto one couple in that world was born a male child who, by obeying his god's laws, would grow into manhood. His death would redeem that world and his resurrection would assure for him his own title of "God."

5. This God, called Elohim or Heavenly Father by Mormons, was then given his own world to organize. He and his celestial wife or wives procreated billions of "spirit children" and tutored them in the heavens.

6. These spirit children were made from the same eternal matter as were all previous worlds and peoples. They were not made from nothing, but from "eternal parts."

7. The first of these children to be made was "Jehovah," later to be known as Jesus Christ. Lucifer was his younger spirit brother, and each of us is his spirit brother or sister.

8. At some point, the gods called a council to determine how best to make gods out of these billions of spirit children. Apparently, this process was not already worked out by previous gods. Each spirit child would have to assume a physical body, live on a mortal earth, be tested, and die. Their performance while in mortality (called their "second estate" to distinguish it from their spirit existence before earthly birth) would determine their status in the future eternity (their "third estate").

9. Christ and Lucifer responded with plans. Christ proposed that all men be given free agency (free will). He would be born a man, would teach and organize a church, and then suffer a redeeming death so that all who accepted him would be saved. By this plan, not all God's spirit children would be assured of returning to heaven after death. Lucifer countered by offering to save all people through depriving them of free will and thus preventing them from sinning.

10. The gods chose Christ's plan. Enraged, Lucifer rebelled and was joined by one-third of the spirit children. They were cast out from the Lord's presence into "outer darkness." They would thus never be born and receive physical bodies, so they have no chance of salvation.

11. Of the remaining two-thirds of the spirits, many fought valiantly for Christ and are rewarded by being born into happy, prosperous families. Those who were least valiant, or even neutral, during the war in heaven, have been assigned less noble parentage. In fact, some are "cursed" with dark skin:

> [A]mong the Saints [i.e., Mormons] is the most likely place for these [choice] spirits to take their tabernacles [human bodies], through a just and righteous parentage. They are to be sent to that people that are the most righteous of any other people upon the earth. . . . The Lord has not kept them in store for five or six thousand years past, and kept them waiting for their bodies all this time to send them among the Hottentots, the African negroes, the idolatrous Hindoos, or any other of the fallen nations that dwell upon the face of this earth. They are not kept in reserve in order to come forth to receive such a degraded parentage upon the earth [Apostle Orson Pratt, *JD* 1:62–63].

12. Elohim and Jehovah took Michael, a pre-existent spirit (Catholics call him an archangel) and gave him a human body. He was now called Adam. From him and Eve the rest of the human population arose.

13. During earthly life, each person has the chance to accept or reject the Mormon "gospel." Those who do so are blessed with the knowledge that, in their pre-existence, they were on the side of Christ. Here, they are expected to live out their pre-mortal commitment.

14. At death, each human spirit enters the "spirit world." Some will go to paradise, others to spirit prison. Their time there will be temporary.

15. Except for a very few, most humans will eventually enjoy some type of heavenly bliss. Even murderers, adulterers, and idolaters who die unrepentant will make it to the

lowest level of heaven. But worthy Mormons will become gods themselves and repeat the above process.

For some reason, Mormons often speak as if theirs is the only church that answers the questions "Where did I come from?" "Why am I here?" and "Where am I going?" Their response is the just-outlined "plan of salvation." Since only the Mormon church teaches such notions, it must be the one, true church. All other churches lead men away from God and therefore are of the devil. This belief, perhaps coupled with more mundane, personal reasons, gives the impetus to the vast proselytizing effort of the Mormon church. Only by joining and remaining faithful to it can you hope to see God again.

A Note on Pre-existence

The idea that all spirit and matter, including the human soul, has an existence independent of and prior to its earthly formation is an essential part of Mormon cosmology. To bolster their assertions, Mormon scholars point to several biblical texts:

> Before I formed thee in the belly I knew thee; and before thou camest forth out of the womb I sanctified thee, and I ordained thee a prophet unto the nations [Jer. 1:5].

Mormons forget that God is all-knowing and all-present. He has foreknowledge of all events, including the calling of a prophet. With this verse and others like it, you need to show Mormons the difference between "ideal" existence and "real" existence. You may, for example, have an idea of what your dream house would be like. In that way, the house "exists" in your mind, as an idea. Only when you build your house does the house have a "real" existence. In the same way, Jeremiah—and each of us—has an eternal "ideal" existence in the mind of God. Not until he created us as beings separate from his idea did we take on "real" existence. (See also Romans 4:17.)

Then shall the dust return to the earth as it was: and the spirit shall return unto God who gave it [Eccl. 12:7].

Mormons read too much into this passage. The "dust" is the human body, which dissolves back to its material elements. The "spirit" is the soul that returns to God who gave it when he created it directly. There's nothing here about an eternally existent human spirit. (See also Acts 17:29.)

[S]hall we not much rather be in subjection unto the Father of spirits, and live? [Heb. 12:9].

Here, the writer emphasizes the immediacy of the creation of the soul. While the formation of a man's body involves the co-operative act of God and two parents, man's soul is created directly and immediately by God alone. In that way, it is fitting to metaphorically call him the "Father of spirits." He made them.

The Catholic Plan of Salvation

1. Where did we come from? "The world was made for the glory of God. . . . The ultimate purpose of creation is that God who is the creator of all things may at last become 'all in all.'" God wanted to make his creatures share in his being, wisdom and goodness [CCC 293–295].

2. Why are we here? "God enables men to be intelligent and free causes in order to complete the work of creation, to perfect its harmony for their own good and that of their neighbors." We enter into the divine plan by our actions, prayers and sufferings [CCC 307]. And we were made "to know, love, and serve God in this life, and be happy with him in the next" [Baltimore Catechism 3, 4].

3. Where are we going? "Those who die in God's grace and friendship and are perfectly purified live for ever with

Christ. . . . Heaven is the ultimate end and fulfillment of the deepest human longings, the state of supreme, definitive happiness. . . . In the glory of heaven the blessed continue joyfully to fulfill God's will in relation to other men and to all creation. Already they reign with Christ; with him 'they shall reign for ever and ever'" [*CCC* 1023, 1024, 1029].

One Mormon Prophet's Explanation of Race Differences:

There is a reason why one man is born black and with other disadvantages, while another is born white with great advantages. The reason is that we once had an estate before we came here, and were obedient, more or less, to the laws that were given us there. Those who were faithful in all things there received greater blessings here, and those who were not faithful received less [Joseph Fielding Smith, *DS* 1:61].

Further reading: CCC 295–314, 355–367, 846–848; *IM*, chapters 22 and 24; *TB*, chapters 7, 8 and 9.

20. Prayer

(*Use for Discussion 1*)

"Since this is your house, and you are its head, would you like to offer a prayer?"

Missionaries or other Mormon visitors typically will ask you this, knowing that you probably would feel too shy or uncomfortable to offer a "spontaneous" prayer. So they will, at least until you get the knack of it.

Mormon Prayer: Do's and Don'ts

Mormons avoid almost any kind of printed, formal, or memorized prayer. The few exceptions are the prayers said over the bread and water at sacrament meetings and the ritualistic words of the temple ceremonies, which aren't really prayer at all. These must be stated exactly or restarted from the beginning.

Instead, they prefer to be "moved by the Holy Ghost" and speak the words they believe he is inspiring them to say. Though Mormons call their prayer spontaneous, it must follow a certain structure:

1. Fold your arms, bow your head, and close your eyes.

2. Always begin by addressing the Heavenly Father. (Mormons are forbidden to pray to Christ or the Holy Spirit, or any saint.)

3. Always use the expressions "thee," "thy," "thou," etc. in addressing God.

4. Continue your prayer by thanking God for whatever gifts you have experienced.

5. Then make your petitions known.

6. Finally, conclude in the name of Jesus Christ.

Missing from this format is any direct praise or adoration of the Lord. In my time as an active Mormon, I rarely remember any public prayer extolling God's goodness and glory. While this attitude may be implicitly present in the Mormons' thanks, it's not insisted upon. The same is true for another element of Christian prayer, contrition or sorrow for sin. This is not to say Mormons do not adore God or ask his forgiveness. They do. But not normally during public prayer.

How Should We Pray?

Catholics pray as the Lord taught. The "Lord's Prayer" summarizes the Christian's attitude toward prayer. Unlike the Mormon model, the "Our Father" teaches us to adore God publicly and explicitly. We are also to ask for help in doing his will. And we petition him for forgiveness. If you're asked to offer a prayer by your Mormon visitors, you couldn't do better than the Lord's own prayer. If you're in a witnessing frame of mind yourself, you could add another biblical prayer, such as the Hail Mary.

Apostle Bruce R. McConkie on Praying to Christ:

This is plain sectarian nonsense. Our prayers are addressed to the Father, and to him only. They do not go through Christ, or the Blessed Virgin, or St. Genevieve or along the beads of a rosary ["Our Relationship with the Lord," 20].

Further reading: CCC 2558–2567, 2623–2699.

21. The Priesthood

(*Use for Discussion 3*)

Priesthood is the keys and authority to properly act and speak in the name of the Lord [President Anthony W. Ivins, *CR*, October 1926, 21].

Mormons say their two priesthoods mirror those that Christ instituted but which were lost to the world because of the general apostasy of the Christian church.

According to the Mormon scripture Doctrine and Covenants (84), the Aaronic or "lesser" priesthood was returned to the earth by John the Baptist on May 15, 1829, who conferred it on Smith and Oliver Cowdery. Within a month or so, the Melchizedek or "greater" priesthood was conferred on them by Peter, James, and John. In both of these priesthood bestowals, Mormonism's fundamental inability to come to grips with the teaching of Scripture is revealed.

The Aaronic Priesthood

In the Old Testament, only the descendants of Moses' brother Aaron could possess the Aaronic priesthood. That's *why* it's called the Aaronic or Levitical priesthood. (Aaron was of the tribe of Levi.) In contrast, the Mormon church confers this preparatory priesthood on people who have no relation to Aaron, on any worthy male member at least twelve years of age. The Mormon "Aaronic priesthood" is not Aaronic at all!

Within Mormonism's "Aaronic priesthood" there are four offices:

1. *Deacon:* Boys aged 12 or 13. These youngsters usually pass the bread and water in Sunday meetings. They also go house-to-house to collect offerings from members.

2. *Teacher:* Boys aged 14 to 15. To their duties as deacon are added the tasks of preparing the bread and water for Sunday meetings, as well as visiting members' homes once a month with an adult male member to impart a spiritual lesson.

3. *Priest:* Boys aged 16 to 17. A "priest" may baptize a new member. He also "blesses" the bread and water and he may "ordain" other priests, teachers, and deacons.

4. *Bishop:* Though technically an elder and high priest, the bishop, as head of the temporal affairs of his congregation, presides over the ward's Aaronic priesthood.

For a detailed explanation of the ways in which these Mormon offices fail to correspond to the biblical offices with the same names, see *Inside Mormonism: What Mormons* Really *Believe*, chapter 5.

The Melchizedek Priesthood

In Scripture there is no such thing as a "Melchizedek priesthood." Melchizedek was a particular priest-king of Jerusalem before the Israelites came into the Land. Since this was also before the founding of the Aaronic priesthood (and before Aaron was even born), Melchizedek was not a member of the Aaronic priesthood. He is later mentioned in Scripture as a comparison to Christ, to show that not all priests have to come from the line of Aaron (though all *Aaronic* priests *do* have to come from the line of Aaron).

Unfortunately, when the King James Version makes the comparison of Christ to Melchizedek, it says "Thou *art* a priest for ever after the order of Melchizedek" (Ps. 110:4b; this Messianic psalm is applied to Christ in Hebrews 5:6, 10, 6:20, 7:11, 7:17). The term "order" is an unfortunate translation that led Mormons into thinking that there was an ecclesiastical order of "Melchizedek priests" comparable to the order of Aaronic priests. There wasn't. The Hebrew term *dibra*, which the King James Version translates as "order," *never* has the sense of an ecclesiastical order; it *never* denotes an organized group of priests, monks, virgins, Nazirites. Instead, it simply means "cause," "reason," or "manner." When the psalm speaks of someone being a priest "after the order of Melchizedek," it means "after the *manner* of Melchizedek" or simply "like Melchizedek." Thus the New American Bible better renders the verse, "The Lord has sworn and will not waver: 'Like Melchizedek you are a priest forever.'"

The New Testament compares Christ to Melchizedek in that he is a genuine priest of God who is not of the line of Aaron and who has no fixed term of office but who always remains a priest. (Other non-Levitical priests included Jethro, Moses' father-in-law, who was a priest of Midian that sacrificed to God; Ex. 18:11–12.)

In the Mormon church, the so-called "Melchizedek priesthood" is composed of two groups.

1. *Elder:* All worthy men about 18 years of age or older may qualify. Male missionaries are in this category. A man receives this designation by the laying on of hands by a man having the proper authority. One who holds this priesthood acts for God within his own sphere of influence. As a husband and father, for instance, he has the right to rule his wife and children with divine inspiration and assistance.

2. *High priest:* This title is reserved to older men or to those who have made significant contributions of service. From this group are chosen the Seventies and the Apostles.

For more information on the ways in which these Mormon offices fail to correspond to the biblical positions bearing the same name, as well as more information on the non-existence of a "Melchizedek order," see *Inside Mormonism: What Mormons Really Believe*, chapter 5.

Where Does It Say All This?

The Mormon church insists that its structure and offices replicate those of the New Testament Church. They do not. An even cursory glance at the Church in Acts and the epistles gives no evidence of boy-priests or "priests" who do everything but offer sacrifice.

For example, according to Paul's first letter to Timothy, deacons should be "grave, not doubletongued, not given to much wine. . . ." They should be "found blameless," and be "the husbands of one wife, ruling their children and their own houses well" (1 Tim. 3:8, 10, 12).

Though Mormons use New Testament designations for their various offices, they redefine them. Still others they omit. For example, where are the Mormon "evangelists" and "pastors"? They have no positions bearing these early-Church titles.

Blacks and the Priesthood

Young and every prophet until 1978 taught that blacks were forbidden to hold the Mormon priesthood. Anyone with even "a drop" of Negro blood was affected.[1] This, members were taught, was God's will because of the lack of obedience and fervor—in the pre-existence—of those born as Negroes in this life.

Faced with intense internal and external opposition to this racist position, Spencer W. Kimball, twelfth Mormon prophet, finally gave in and said it was revealed to him by the Lord that all wor-

---

[1] Young, cited by Mormon apostle Matthias F. Cowley, in Jerald and Sandra Tanner, *Mormons and Negroes*, 10.

thy male members should receive the blessings of the priesthood and the temple. His divine "revelation," presented to the church on September 30, 1978, thus nullified the teachings of all of his predecessors regarding whether blacks could hold the Mormon priesthoods, but it did not change the teaching that people are born Negro as a punishment for misdeeds in the pre-existence.

The True Priesthood Offers Sacrifice

Ask your Mormon friend what "priesthood" means and he will give you the answer presented at the beginning of this topic. But that is a Mormon re-definition. It's akin to their reworking of the meaning of "one God," or "virgin" or "gospel." True priesthood offers sacrifice (Heb. 5:1, 8:3). For that reason alone, the Mormon church does not possess a true priesthood. Its leaders offer no sacrifice, and would in fact cringe at the thought. Mormon "priesthood" holders join the vast number of Protestant leaders who "minister" to the spiritual needs of their people, without once doing for them the one thing necessary: offering the sacrifice of the Mass for their salvation and God's glory.

Further reading: CCC 1536–1600; *IM*, chapters 3–5; *TB*, chapters 13 and 14.

22. Prophets

(*Use for Discussions 1 and 6*)

"I never told you I was perfect; but there is no error in the revelations which I have taught" (Joseph Smith, *HC* 6:366). The Mormon church calls its leadership "prophets" and "apostles." These men, from such fields as business, education, and law, are said to be chosen by God to lead his church. All are considered to be "prophets, seers, and revelators" to the Mormon church.

Only the prophet, the President of the Mormon church, has the right to speak in God's name to the entire membership. When he proclaims a "revelation," the church is obligated to hear and obey. Mormons say that no other major faith professes to be led by direct divine revelation. This is open to debate. For example, the Assemblies of God is a major Pentecostal body that believes that frequent divine revelation is given to its members, including its leaders.

Does the Bible Provide for Prophets?

Mormons insist Christ's church must be led by prophets. They point to Amos 3:7, which states: "Surely the Lord GOD will do nothing, but he revealeth his secret unto his servants the prophets." This verse will not support the Mormon model for prophets and prophecy. If it proved anything, it would prove too much.

Amos was in the process of prophesying disaster befalling the northern kingdom of Israel. This was the context for his saying that God doesn't (from today's perspective: *didn't*) do anything without telling the prophets first so that they could announce it to the people. But do Mormon prophets claim to be informed about every calamity that impacts their sphere? Do they announce it beforehand to the Mormon people so they can repent and avoid it, as the biblical prophets did? Do they announce them as disasters brought on the Mormon people because of their sins—or do they announce no calamity at all and praise the Mormon people for their allegedly superior uprightness?

More fundamentally the age for new, publicly binding revelation is over. Hebrews 1:1–2 states:

> In times past, God spoke in fragmentary and varied ways to our fathers through the prophets; in this, the final age, he has spoken to us through his Son, whom he has made heir of all things [NAB].

False Prophets and Prophecies

Mormons sometimes miss another biblical passage dealing with discernment:

> But the prophet, which shall presume to speak a word in my name, which I have not commanded him to speak, or that shall speak in the name of other gods, even that prophet shall die. . . . When a prophet speaketh in the name of the Lord, if the thing follow not, nor come to pass, that is the thing which the Lord hath not spoken, but the prophet hath spoken it presumptuously: thou shalt not be afraid of him [Deut. 18:20, 22].

Scripture warns us that there will always be false prophets presuming to speak for God.

Further reading: CCC 904–907, 2030–2051; *IM*, chapters 3 and 33; *CF*, chapters 17 and 18.

23. Standard Works

(*Use for Discussion 3*)

We believe the Bible to be the word of God as far as it is translated correctly; we also believe the Book of Mormon to be the word of God [Articles of Faith, 8].

Mormons and the Bible

In the past, the Mormon church offered free copies of its Book of Mormon to anyone who asked. Currently, the Mormons will give you a free copy of the King James Version of the Bible, complete with Mormon footnotes and cross-references. This is odd, on the face of it, since the Mormon church's position on the Bible is that it is flawed and incomplete. Early apostle Orson Pratt said,

> [T]he Bible has been robbed of its plainness; many sacred books having been lost, others rejected by the Romish [Catholic] Church, and what few we have left, were copied and re-copied so many times, that it is admitted that almost every verse has been corrupted and mutilated to that degree that scarcely any two of them read alike [*The Seer*, 213].

What Books? Which Verses?

Ask the missionaries how they "feel" about the Bible, and they will "testify" that it is the word of God—to a limited degree. They'll tell you that many books belonging to it were either lost or removed by Catholic leaders. These books were purged, of course, because they supposedly provided a solid basis for Mormon teachings.

When they refer to books mentioned by the Bible itself that we no longer have, don't be confused. The work of the Holy Spirit is not thwarted by the "carelessness" of men (though Mormons believe it is). Lost books were never meant to be part of Sacred Scripture, since we have God's assurance that his word (comprised of both written material and oral tradition) "shall stand forever" (Is. 40:8). Likewise, Christ promised that not a single letter of the divine word would ever pass away (Matt. 5:18).

You should also ask your Mormon friends which verses of the Bible are incorrect. Smith attempted to rewrite the Bible, subtracting and adding single words and even blocks of text to make the original inspired writing conform to his ever-changing doctrinal inventions. What he produced has been called the "Inspired Version" or the "Joseph Smith Translation." No act of translating was involved. Rather, Smith simply read the original biblical text and "intuited" what he figured God had meant it to be. Strangely, though, Smith's version is not used by the Mormon church as its standard Bible, and the Smith revision of Scripture is *not* the one Mormons hand out to prospective converts.

As an aside, you might ask your proselytizers another question.

"If the Catholic Church removed from the Bible all the 'plain and precious parts' you maintain it did, why didn't it take out 1 Corinthians 15:29, the only biblical reference to what you term 'baptism for the dead'? If the passage so clearly indicates that early, orthodox Christians carried on such a practice, don't you think the anti-Mormons would have caught it early on and purged it?

"Furthermore, where are any records from any time period of the Church trying to remove material from Scripture? You won't find any! The Church has always taken great pains to accurately preserve and transmit Scripture. There is no evidence anywhere of Church officials ordering passages struck from the biblical manuscripts—which would be an impossible task anyway, since the manuscripts were either in private hands or waiting for modern archaeology to discover them, in either case, inaccessible to Church leaders."

The Book of Mormon

The second of the "standard works" of Mormons is the Book of Mormon. See the section devoted to it for a fuller examination.

The Doctrine and Covenants

This "standard work" is a collection of 138 sections, most of which are "revelations" Smith said he received from Jesus. Most were written before Smith's death in 1844.

The contents of his Book of Mormon could not support Smith's continual revision of his new religion. Therefore, supplementary divine approval was needed for the strange tenets of many gods and many wives, the conviction that large tracts of American land were the God-given inheritance of Mormons, and such novelties as temples, Aaronic and Melchizedek priesthoods, and mission work among the dead.

Smith even got enough of his followers to believe Christ was speaking to him about how to discern good angels from bad (shake hands with them; D&C 129); whom to appoint as church historian (though the Lord later deposed his earlier choice; D&C 47); and what should happen to surplus property (it was to be given to the Mormon bishops, D&C 119; but when the members rebelled, the Lord reneged).

The Pearl of Great Price

The fourth "standard work" of the Mormon church contains several shorter writings by Joseph Smith.

A. "The Book of Moses" is Smith's rewriting of the first several chapters of Genesis. In it, we learn of the pre-existence of all matter and spirit and the war in heaven. God tells Moses that he taught Adam and Eve the gospel of his Son, baptized them in Christ's name and gave them the Holy Ghost [5:8–9]. Rather than repenting and grieving over their sin, our first parents rejoiced, saying, "Were it not for our transgressions we never should have known good and evil, and the joy of our redemption" [5:11].

B. "Joseph Smith—Matthew" is Smith's reworking of Matthew 24.

C. "Joseph Smith—History" is Smith's account of his early visions and the production of the Book of Mormon.

D. "The Articles of Faith" is a list of thirteen Mormon statements of belief that Smith originally sent to a newspaper editor.

E. "The Book of Abraham" is unique among all Mormon scriptures and the most controversial. It is said to be a supernatural translation of some papyrus records Smith obtained from a traveling salesman of Egyptian mummies and curiosities in 1835. Widespread skepticism regarding the prophet's ability to "translate" the golden plates of the Book of Mormon was therefore to be quieted by Smith's work on the ancient papyrus. Smith reported that, to his amazement, the writings were in the hand of the patriarch Abraham! Though Egyptian had already been deciphered through the efforts of Jean François Champollion (1790–1832) and other early Egyptologists, Smith forged ahead and produced, purportedly under divine inspiration, an account of Abraham's sojourn in Egypt.

Among other novelties, Smith read the patriarch's account of a council of gods at the beginning of creation (chapters 4 and 5). He also found out that the God of this world lives somewhere near the great star Kolob (3:16). Further, Abraham 1:23–27 served, for over 140 years, as a basis for the Mormon refusal to allow blacks the priesthood.

Many innovations Smith had made between the first publication of the Book of Mormon in 1830 and his "translation" of the Abraham papyri in 1835 now found divine ratification. Though the Book of Mormon knows only one God, a spirit, the Book of Abraham teaches a plurality of gods, the chief of whom lives on a star far distant from earth.

The Book of Abraham is unique among Mormon scriptures for its fantastic contents and because we still have the manuscript from which it was "translated." The golden plates from which the Book of Mormon was produced were allegedly taken back by an angel, so their translation cannot be verified. The "revelations" granted Smith in compiling his "inspired version" of the Bible, the Book of Moses and the Doctrine and Covenants were merely subjective impressions and not verifiable by objective analysis. It appeared the same fate attended the Egyptian papyri, which were thought lost in an 1871 fire. But in 1967, Mormon officials made the dramatic announcement that the writings had been discovered and donated to the Mormon church by New York's Metropolitan Museum of Art. Eventually, the Mormon church made copies available to Egyptologists, every one of whom declared them to be part of the Book of the Dead—funeral writings typical of those traditionally buried with mummies from the centuries immediately preceding Christ. Abraham is not mentioned in these pagan writings, and the "gods" referred to are pagan ones. Today, Mormon scholars scurry to find alternative theories for the Book of Abraham's "translation." Until they can convince their membership with objective fact, Mormon leaders must ask them to depend on their subjective testimonies that Smith turned pagan texts into God-breathed scripture.

Further reading: CCC 74–141; *IM*, chapters 27 and 32.

24. Temples

(*Use for Discussion 4*)

Temples are sanctified for the purpose of performing rites for and making covenants with the pure in heart, who have proved themselves by faithful service worthy of the blessings of exaltation [Joseph Fielding Smith, *DS* 2:231].

Only those already "pure in heart" and proven faithful may step inside any of the more than fifty Mormon temples throughout the world. This means, in fact, that only about twenty percent of the world's Mormons are permitted entry.

Who Can Go to the Temple?

Only Mormons in good standing with their church may receive a slip of paper called a "temple recommend" allowing them to enter a temple. To be "in good standing," the member must be interviewed by two local leaders and answer correctly such questions as: Do you pay a full tithe? (Ten percent of income.) Do you observe the Word of Wisdom? (No coffee, tea, tobacco, or alcohol.) Do you obey and support all local and general LDS authorities? Do you attend church meetings faithfully? Do you discharge all church responsibilities carefully? Do you observe chastity? (Though unnatural birth control and marriage after divorce are permitted.) Do you believe all that the LDS church teaches? Do you consider yourself worthy to enter the temple? If the member answers yes to all the questions, he is generally granted a pass to the temple, good for one year. At the end of that time, he must repeat the interview process.

Why Bother with the Temple?

The Mormon church maintains that unless you attend the temple and receive the special instructions offered there, you will not reach the highest level of heaven and be able to become a god yourself. The best you could hope for would be a servant's position in the hereafter. All those who fail to achieve temple status are considered "damned," regardless of the goodness of life they've led.

Mormon scholars assert that, just as their theology and practices faithfully reproduce those of the Old Testament and New Testament believers, so do their temples. If that's true, you might ask the missionaries if animals are sacrificed or sheaves of grain are waved in front of God's ark in the temples. Is incense offered to the Lord? Are there ritual cleansings of vessels and other items? The answer is "no" to each question. You can also ask where in the Bible (or the Book of Mormon, for that matter) there's any discussion of endowment ceremonies, sealings, and underground immersions. There aren't any such places.

People don't go to a Mormon temple for a "visit." They don't go to sit and pray or even to attend worship services. There are no such things in the temples. Rather, worthy members attend mainly to further their own or a dead person's chances for eventual godhood. They attend to learn secret and "sacred" information. Here's how it works:

Temple Ordinances

Temple rituals fall into four categories.

1. *Baptisms for the dead.* This aberrant practice was discussed under "Baptism." A living member (teenagers may qualify) undergoes total immersion baptism in an underground tank that rests on the backs of twelve sculpted

oxen. A proxy may stand in for even ten or twenty persons at a time, being immersed for each one in order. It is thought that, should the dead person accept the Mormon gospel in spirit prison, he posthumously enters the Mormon church, is released from prison, and is sent to paradise, to await further proxy ordinances.

2. *Washings and anointings.* Together with the endowment and sealing ceremonies, these rituals must be received first for oneself but then may be repeated multiple times for the dead. Only adults may participate. Temple washings and anointings have been attacked by some Mormon critics who believe they have prurient, sexual overtones. They don't. The member wears nothing but a white, poncholike cloth shield. A temple worker dabs each part of the member's body with water first, then oil. A rote recitation asking for God's blessing accompanies the actions. There is nothing unseemly or immodest about the ordinance. Afterward, the temple patron dresses in his temple "garments," white underwear similar to a T-shirt and boxer shorts containing small embroidered markings similar to Masonic symbols. Except when bathing, he must wear these day and night for the rest of his life.

3. *The endowment.* To "receive one's endowment," one attends the longest of the temple ordinances. This is done first for oneself; return visits may be made on behalf of the deceased. The endowment involves about 90 minutes of instruction presented in theater-like rooms seating about 150 persons. Through audio, video and even live performances, Mormon views of the creation, fall of man and redemption are acted out. At various times in the program, patrons stand and make certain covenants or promises, including fidelity in marriage, supporting Mormon leadership and using all their resources to further the interests of the Mormon church. Various symbolic garments are also put on and four sets of handclasps, arm

gestures and code names are repeated. These reflect Smith's involvement with Freemasonry at the time he composed the temple rites. All is to be kept secret and never discussed outside the temple.

4. *Sealings.* The Mormons' goal is to provide baptism, washings, anointings, and endowments for every person who ever lived. Further, according to their beliefs, no man can achieve divinity unless he has been sealed to a wife or wives in a Mormon temple. After an earthly husband and wife have themselves been sealed or married in the temple in a brief ritual of making certain promises, they may then stand in as proxies for their dead ancestors. Those who, when alive, had been married are sealed to their earthly spouses. Deceased single people must be sealed in a Mormon marriage if they are to have any chance at becoming gods. Several women may, in fact, be sealed to the same man.

Recall, from the section on "Families," that such eternal sealings may be canceled. Some divorced Mormons, having rid themselves of their earthly spouse, don't fancy the prospect of having him or her back again for all eternity. So they petition the First Presidency to have their temple sealings unsealed.

A second form of sealing is that of children to parents. Children born to a Mormon couple who were sealed as spouses in the temple do not need further sealing. All others do. If a family converts to the Mormon faith, after the parents are sealed the children are brought to the sealing room where a brief statement is made. Or, if my parents are dead, I must be sure they are posthumously baptized and endowed as Mormons, then have them sealed as spouses. After that, I have myself sealed to them. I then repeat the process for my grandparents, great-grandparents, and as far back as I can trace my ancestry. Mormons expect eventually to seal the entire human race, through all generations of time back to Adam and Eve.

The Main Problem with the Temple

Hebrews 1:1 makes it clear that Christ has revealed to his apostles and to us all that we need to believe and do to reach eternal life. Christian scripture and even the Book of Mormon know of no temple like those the Mormons construct and attend. Secret code words and handshakes are meant to get you into a boy's tree house; they are not necessary for salvation.

Rather than praising and adoring Christ and his Father, the temple patron listens to a bland, repetitious program written by Smith (though many changes have been made to his "God-given" text over the years).

The temple has come under attack by some critics who claim its ceremonies are satanic and filled with sexual debauchery. Either these folks have never gone through a Mormon temple or they have lost touch with reality. There is nothing of the sort in the Mormon rituals. But that does touch on what I consider the worst aspect of the temple ordinances. They're not nearly as evil as their opponents say. Nor are they as sublime as the missionaries and other members tell you. They are boring, repetitive, insipid. Temple ordinances are man-made creations, irrelevant to true religion or eternal salvation. Not surprisingly, there are many who, having gone once, never return.

Further reading: IM, chapters 7 and 24.

25. Three Degrees of Glory

(*Use for Discussions 4 and 6*)

The greatest revelation the Lord, Jesus Christ, has ever given to man, so far as record is made, was given to the Prophet Joseph Smith on the 16th of April, 1832, known as the 76th section of the book of *Doctrine & Covenants* [Apostle Melvin J. Ballard, "Three Degrees of Glory," 3–4].

Recall that Smith had received many alleged revelations, including the corporeality of God the Father and the multiplicity of gods. What could be more momentous than that? Apparently, the fact that "heaven" is divided into three distinct tiers, each ruled by ; member of the Mormon Godhead.

The Spirit World

According to the Mormon church, when a person dies, he enter the spirit world. There are two main divisions here: paradise fo worthy Mormons and spirit prison for all others. Both places af ford their residents the time and opportunity to grow spirituall and make choices. Most important, the spirits of dead Mormon are permitted to leave paradise and travel to spirit prison. There, they carry on missionary work similar to that conducted on earth.

Spirits in prison have the chance to hear the missionary discussions and accept or reject the "gospel." Should they accept, they must await the proxy work done by a living Mormon on their behalf. After that, they are freed from prison and enter paradise. There, through the process of "eternal progression," the faithful Mormon learns all things necessary to become a god himself.

The Resurrection of the Body

Mormons believe in a literal 1000-year reign of Jesus Christ upon the earth. When he returns, dead Mormons who had achieved the highest levels of obedience will be raised to rule with him. Resurrections will continue throughout the millennium, with murderers and other serious sinners rising last.

Three Heavens?

Mormonism teaches that heaven is divided into three primary levels. Support for this notion comes from Paul's first letter to the Corinthians:

> There are also celestial bodies, and bodies terrestrial: but the glory of the celestial is one, and the glory of the terrestrial is another. There is one glory of the sun, and another glory of the moon, and another glory of the stars. . . . So also is the resurrection of the dead. It is sown in corruption; it is raised in incorruption [1 Cor. 15:40–42].

Mormons believe Paul teaches three separate degrees of glory: of the sun, moon, and stars. Each person will be given his place among one of those degrees. Mormons call such places the celestial, the terrestrial, and the telestial kingdoms. (Smith simply made up this last term by running the first two together.)

All of chapter 15 deals with the resurrection—Christ's and ours. In these verses, Paul answers the question, "How are the dead raised up? and with what body do they come?" (15:35). His response is that the mortal body is buried in its corruptible state but comes forth in glorious immortality. And just as heavenly bodies (sun, moon, and stars, or "celestial") differ in glory from earth's ("terrestrial"), so too does the glorified human body differ from the mortal one. Nothing is said here about kingdoms of heaven.

Even when Paul speaks of the sun, moon, and stars, he does not speak of three levels of glory, for each star has its own level of brightness, "for one star differeth from another star in glory" (1 Cor. 15:41). Paul's point is that there is a spectrum of different glories exemplified by the objects we see in the sky.

Who attains each level?

1. *Celestial kingdom:* This is reserved to fully faithful Mormons who have received their temple endowments. God the Father rules here, and those who enter are said to have returned to him. This degree, itself, is subdivided into three levels. The highest level is eternal life and is reserved to those who have been sealed in the temple. Those who achieve it will become gods of their own worlds. The Mormon man and his wife or wives will procreate spirit children and place them into the bodies of humans who will populate the new earths they will rule. In turn, their children will adore these new gods just as we currently worship the Heavenly Father. The second level is undefined at present. The third level is for those faithful Mormons who were never sealed to spouses and are therefore barred from future progression. They eternally will be servants to the married gods and goddesses.

2. *Terrestrial kingdom:* Most "good" people will reside in this degree of glory. They include Mormons who did not live up to every obligation and promise, together with the holy people of other faiths. We assume, for example, that Mother Teresa supposedly would go here (unless, of course, spirit missionaries were able to convince her after death to convert to the Mormon church). Jesus Christ rules here, and the Father does not visit. Though it is hard to imagine, Smith actually named this kingdom "terrestrial," as if he didn't know the proper meaning of that word, which is "earthly." Here on earth, we are *already* living in the only thing that can be properly called the "terrestrial" kingdom.

3. *Telestial kingdom:* According to Mormon commentators, most of mankind ends up here. "Liars and sorcerers, and adulterers, and whoremongers, and whosoever loves and makes a lie" will be found here, enjoying a glory "which surpasses all understanding" (D&C 76:89, 103). Those who never knew Christ or had rejected him are raised to telestial glory and have the Holy Ghost as their ruler.

It's possible, Mormons say, to progress within a kingdom, but no one can make the leap from a lower degree of glory to the next higher.

This scheme effectively denies the reality of an eternal hell. While those in the lower degrees may have to suffer some temporal cleansing and punishment, once this is completed they are brought into glory and happiness unimaginable. The only "damnation" they experience is a "damming" of their eternal procession towards godhood. But even the lowest kingdom, where those who die unrepentant ultimately reside, is filled with joy and peace. Selfish men of earth won't see that as too bad a deal.

Outer Darkness

There is one place devoid of glory. Lucifer, his spirit followers and a very few humans (Mormons say Cain, for example) will be eternally lost. They have no share in any happiness (though some Mormons theorize that even these may ultimately be "saved"). This outer darkness is also reserved for those Mormons who, having been convinced of Mormon truth, turned their backs on it.

Further reading: CCC 992–1060; *IM,* chapters 24–26; *TB,* chapters 19 and 20; *CF,* chapter 16.

26. Tithing

(*Use for Discussion 5*)

Before joining the Mormon church you must promise to pay the church ten percent of your income. If you won't make this covenant, you're refused baptism. Baptized members who later renege on payments are forbidden entry into the Mormon temples and will not progress to higher positions in the church. The unbaptized and the unfaithful are denied eternal life. The most they can hope for is a secondary status outside the presence of the Heavenly Father. Not paying a sufficient tithe is a major factor in barring the majority of members from temple attendance.

Citing such verses as Malachi 3:8–11 and Hebrews 7:1–2, Mormons make a valid point about supporting the church with financial offerings and gifts in kind. As Catholics, we recognize that we have a moral duty to support our faith and worthy charitable works. But the size of our contributions is not set down by law in the Christian age. We must use our conscience and common sense.

Unlike the Mormon church, the Catholic Church does not deny its greatest blessings and thus punish people who do not pay a predetermined quota.

Uses of Tithes

First, tithes are spent on the vast work of expanding the Mormon church. On the average, one new Mormon meeting house is erected each day. In addition, the Mormon church has begun a plan of building smaller but more temples. These buildings are raised only after being paid for with tithing funds. Missionary and publication work is financed though members' tithes. Mormon leaders are also paid from tithing income.

Second, tithes are occasionally used in charitable works. Usually, however, the Mormon welfare system is run on yet additional, required offerings from the membership. For example, once a month, generally on the first Sunday, each Mormon is told to give up two meals. The money thus saved is collected and put into the local congregation's welfare fund.

Finally, tithing benefits the person tithing. Only those who pay a full tithe will be called to any position of honor or leadership. This is not to say that those who pay will advance; full tithers must obey all the other rules of the church as well. It is a certainty, though, that those who do not pay their tithes will not grow in the esteem of either God or the Mormon church.

Further reading: CCC 2041–2043, 2419–2436.

27. Word of Wisdom

(*Use for Discussion 4*)

[The Word of Wisdom] is given as a commandment; the Word of Wisdom did proceed from the mouth of God to us as a people, and as the will of the Lord, and therefore we are under a command to observe it [Apostle Marvin O. Ashton, *CR*, Oct. 1938, 57].

Spittoons and Revelations

The elders of the early Mormon church used to meet in a room over Joseph and Emma Smith's house in Kirtland, Ohio. After a good deal of pipe smoking, they would take large chews of tobacco and "spit all over the floor." Smith's wife was none too pleased with having to clean up the mess, and Smith quieted her by "inquiring of the Lord." The revelation known as the Word of Wisdom was given by Christ on Feb. 27, 1833. As a "principle of promise," the Lord forbade consuming alcohol, tobacco or "hot drinks" (deemed by later prophets to refer to hot or cold coffee or tea and eventually extended to cover caffeinated colas). Meat was to be eaten sparingly, and then only in winter and times of famine. (This is no longer observed.) Grains and vegetables were especially commended. Those who followed this divine counsel would "find wisdom and great treasures of knowledge." (See D&C 89.)

At first the "Word of Wisdom" was presented only as advice, not as having the force of law for Mormons. But the "advice" from God soon took on the status of a commandment. For decades, now, members have been asked in their yearly interviews with church authorities if they keep the Word of Wisdom. Failure to do so—

except for the meat prohibition, which has silently fallen through the cracks—bars one from attending the temple and from church leadership positions.

One Mormon historian maintains the Word of Wisdom was "raised" to the status of a commandment under Young, who didn't want to see the Utah Saints' money leaving the territory in exchange for the imported tobacco, liquor, coffee, and tea. The implementation of the revelation was, then, for mainly economic reasons—to protect the viability of the new Mormon enterprise (Leonard Arrington, *BYU Studies*, Winter 1959, 43).

While Paul does urge moderation (Phil. 4:5), he stands fast in maintaining that all foods are to be received with thanksgiving: "For everything created by God is good, and nothing is to be rejected if it is received with thanksgiving" (1 Tim. 4:4, RSV). Specifically, as a matter of Christian liberty, Paul commands us not to accept the idea that some kinds of food are religiously "better" or more holy than others: "Let no man therefore judge you in meat, or in drink" (Col. 2:16). This includes even alcohol, so long as moderation is observed. Rather than condemn the consumption of alcohol, for example, the Bible clearly permits and even advises it (1 Tim. 3:8, 5:23; Tit. 2:3; 1 Pet. 4:3; also Deut. 14:24–26; Prov. 31:6–7).

Further reading: CCC 2290.

Afterword:
"I Will Be Like the Most High"?

by James Akin

God himself was once as we are now, and is an exalted man, and sits enthroned in yonder heavens! That is the great secret. If the veil were rent today . . . you would see him like a man in form like yourselves in all the person, image, and very form as a man. . . . Here, then, is eternal life—to know the only wise and true God; and you have got to learn how to be gods yourselves [Joseph Smith, *King Follett Discourse*, April 7, 1844].

The central claim of the Mormon church—that men and women can become the deities of their own worlds, the same as God the Father now is, with billions worshiping them—represents the ambition of Lucifer, who said in his heart, "I will ascend above the heights of the clouds; I will be like the Most High" (Is. 14:14). To such aspirations, the biblical response can only be, "Yet thou shalt be brought down to hell, to the sides of the pit" (Is. 14:15). The devil has craved worship and equality with God ever since he fell. So consumed with this desire is he that he was willing to surrender his dark control of the pagan nations of the world if the Lord Jesus would only fall down and worship him (Matt. 4:8–9).

When not directly encouraging people to worship him, the devil has encouraged others to gradually come under his sway by following his example, by falling from grace through aspiring to be like God. This was the original lie he told Adam and Eve— that death would not come to them if they aspired to "be as gods" (Gen. 3:4–5). This was the lie that, once believed and acted upon, caused the fall of the human race.

It also is the lie that the Mormon church wishes its members to believe and act upon. This may shock some, but it is the truth. There is a time for being polite and a time for being diplomatic, but there is also a time for plain speaking. The fact is: The Mormon church's "evangelization" efforts serve to spread the original lie that Satan told in the Garden. The Mormon church tries to inspire people with Luciferian ambitions.

The Mormon hierarchy has spent a great deal of effort trying to reinvent Mormonism in the public mind, to change its negative image from the nineteenth century to a positive one. They wish Mormonism to be seen as a positive, "mainstream" Christian church. But no matter how much Christian terminology is co-opted and redefined, no matter how many television and radio advertisements are bought, no matter how often bicycling missionaries assure their hearers that Mormonism is authentically Christian, the fact cannot be changed that the Mormon religion is not only not Christian in its beliefs, but that it is founded on deep spiritual darkness.

It is the duty of all Christians, therefore, to resist the efforts of the Mormon hierarchy to portray their organization as if it were a mainstream, authentic expression of Christianity. It is not. Its core message represents the very antithesis of Christianity. The Mormon "gospel" of becoming gods is the lie of Satan, and thus the *opposite* of the Good News of Jesus Christ, who came to *rescue* us from that lie's consequences.

If you are a Mormon reading this, you must cast off the deceptions that have been passed on to you by the Mormon hierarchy. The fact that it is laboring to spread the lie of the Garden proves that, no matter how good and pious it seeks outwardly to appear, inwardly it is controlled by spiritual darkness. Paul's words regarding false apostles of his day apply equally well to the "apostles" of Mormonism:

[S]uch men are false apostles, deceitful workmen, disguising themselves as apostles of Christ. And no wonder, for even Satan disguises himself as an angel of light. So it is not strange if his servants also disguise themselves as servants of righteousness. Their end will correspond to their deeds [2 Cor. 11:13–15].

If you are a Mormon, *your end* must not be allowed to correspond to theirs. Changing one's faith can be a great strain, but you must save your soul, and to do that you *must* reject the lie that you, a creature of the one true God, could aspire to be "as God now is." You must realize that worship is due only to the infinite, all holy Creator and that his finite creatures must not aspire to one day offer themselves as objects of divine adoration.

It is essential to recognize the lie of the Garden for what it is, to turn from it, and to embrace the historic Christian faith. As Mormons recognize, Jesus founded a visible Church on earth and gave it the authority to speak and exercise ministry in his name. But he also gave this Church the Holy Spirit and promised that his presence would remain with it forever, saying, "Lo, I am with you always, even unto the end of the world" (Matt. 28:20).

Speaking to Peter, Jesus solemnly swore, "And I say also unto thee, That thou art Peter, and upon this rock I will build my Church; and the gates of hell shall not prevail against it" (Matt. 16:18). Mormons rightly recognize that, in making these promises, Jesus made Peter the head of the Church in his absence. What they fail to consider is that Jesus indicated he would have only one Church—described as "my Church"—and that the gates of hell would not prevail against it.

This means that the Church Jesus put Peter in charge of was "his Church"—the one true Church. There would be no second Church founded in the New World, nor would there be a third Church founded in America in the 1800s. Why? Because Jesus promised that the gates of hell would not prevail against the Church he founded upon Peter. If that Church had begun to teach heresy, apostatized, fallen away from Christ, and disappeared from the earth then the gates of hell *would* have prevailed against it. Since we have Jesus' solemn promise that that would not happen, we know that the Church Jesus founded on Peter never fell.

So it is no surprise when we discover that there is one single communion of Christians that has lived through all these centuries, that was founded on Peter, that has never had the gates of hell prevail against it, and that is shepherded by the successor of Peter today. That Church is the Catholic Church, and that Church is the one you must join if you wish to obey the will of Christ.

Ultimately, it comes down to a question of trust. Who are you going to trust more? Jesus Christ or Joseph Smith? The two are not in agreement. In his day, Jesus Christ raised the standards of morality, including sexual morality (Mark 10:1–12), and he himself lived chastely; Joseph Smith lessened the rules of sexual morality for his own benefit, introducing polygamy after he impregnated a young female houseguest (pp. 68–69). Jesus Christ proclaimed the word of God and gave all of his teachings in public (John 18:20); Joseph Smith hid key rituals of his new religion (pp. 127–131) and claimed to have access to secret scriptures that nobody was allowed to see except with "the eyes of faith" (pp. 46–47).

Jesus Christ promised that the single Church he founded would never die but would always remain upon the earth (Matt. 16:18); Joseph Smith said Jesus founded two Churches, both of which failed and perished from the earth when the gates of hell prevailed against them (pp. 27–28). Jesus Christ died a martyr's death, not resisting those who were unjustly putting him to death (Is. 53:7, Matt. 27:12–14); Joseph Smith died shooting a firearm in a jailhouse gun battle, following his arrest for ordering the destruction of a newspaper critical of him (p. 97). Jesus said the serpent was a liar and the father of lies (John 8:44); Joseph Smith told his followers to believe the lie of the serpent—that they can become as gods (p. 134).

One cannot believe both Jesus Christ and Joseph Smith. Their lives, their credibility, and their messages are diametrically opposed. The question is: Which are *you* going to believe? Which are *you* going to trust with your immortal soul?